The EU: The Truth about the Fourth Reich

How Adolf Hitler Won the Second World War

Daniel J. Beddowes and Flavio Cipollini

Contents

Important Dates in the History of the EU

1933: Benito Mussolini talks of the need for political unity in Europe.

1936: Adolf Hitler devises the name "United States of Europe" to describe his plan for a united Europe.

1940: Walther Funk, economics adviser to Hitler, prepares a memo entitled "Economic Reorganisation of Europe" and proposes a standard European currency.

1942: Reinhard Heydrich, architect of the Holocaust, publishes "The Reich Plan for the Domination of Europe" (a precursor of The Treaty of Rome).

1943: Thirteen countries are invited to join a new European Federation under German military control.

1944: A Nazi conference is held in Strasbourg (now the headquarters of the EU) to discuss how Germany will dominate the peace after the war ends.

1952: The European Coal and Steel Community is created.

1957: The Rome Treaty is signed and the European Economic Community is founded.

1973: British Prime Minister Edward Heath takes Britain into the Common Market. He receives £35,000 tax free.

Part One: Why We're All Living in a Foreign Country

Thanks to the EU we face a future without democracy, justice, equality, peace, freedom or privacy. Thanks to the EU our responsibilities are increasing at the same rate as our rights are disappearing. It is thanks to the EU that the quality of health care, education and transport has fallen dramatically. If you are concerned at the poor quality of police services or council facilities you can blame the EU. If you are upset that your library has closed and your street is constantly full of rubbish you can thank the EU. It is difficult to think of any aspect of our lives which has not been adversely affected by the EU and it is impossible to think of any way in which the EU has contributed in a positive way to our health, wealth or well-being. It is the EU we must thank for the barrage of new laws which make life miserable and the vast amount of red tape which makes life ever more difficult. It is the EU which is responsible for making travel difficult and sometimes intolerable and it is the EU which is responsible for the fact that opening a bank account is almost as difficult as moving your own money when you've opened one. People tend to blame the Government for all these things but the truth is that it isn't the Government's fault. Politicians don't like to admit it (indeed, they often play a curious game with the electorate by threatening to stop new EU laws but they've sold our country, and Parliament no longer has any control over what happens in Britain. (Politicians are, indeed, told that they cannot blame the EU for `bad laws'. In 1971 the Foreign Office published a document entitled FCO 30/1048. Paragraph 24 advises politicians that there is `major responsibility on HMG and on all political parties not to exacerbate public concern by attributing unpopular measures or unfavourable economic details to remote and unmanageable workings of the Community.')

Every Prime Minister from Edward Heath onwards has betrayed the people of Britain and since all three major political parties have supported these betrayals no one in Westminster now dares admit just how much power has been given away. Our country is run by unelected, foreign eurocrats who are overcome with conceit and a conviction that they always know best and who suppress democracy and impose their will upon the people of Europe without ever allowing their malignant megalomania to be disrupted for a moment by good sense, respect or compassion. Like all true fascists these eurocrats are forever eager to follow the guidelines set down by Mussolini and Hitler, and to continue to meld corporate power with political power to the direct benefit of those involved.

There is much confusion about fascism. Curiously, the Europhiles claim that anyone who opposes the EU, Hitler's dream, must be a fascist but it isn't difficult to prove that this is simply a rather crude form of mis-direction. (`What good fortune for governments,' said Hitler, `that the people do not think.') The one important thing to remember is that fascism was invented by Mussolini in 1919 and his definition is quite simple: `Liberalism denied the state in the name of the individual,' he said, `fascism reasserts the rights of the state as expressing the real essence of the individual.' Mussolini went on to argue that: `the more complicated the forms of civilisation, the more restricted the freedom of the individual must become.' It is clear from these simple comments that the European Union is a truly fascist organisation. The EU reduces our freedom and our privacy because only the state really matters; the rights and needs of the state (the EU) take precedence over the rights and needs of the citizens.

And so it is not really an accident that the EU has wrecked life in every conceivable way. The fact is that the EU (and the people who run it) don't believe in the rights of individuals but they do believe in the rights of the organisation they represent. (Naturally, however, the undistinguished individuals who run the EU also realise that their power gives them a very welcome opportunity to make money for themselves. Their individual rights have flourished in the fascist environment the EU has created.)

The EU is responsible for the introduction of all day drinking, absurd laws about rubbish disposal, the regionalisation of the police, unlimited immigration, sex education for the under 13s, the running down of British manufacturing, the costly privatisation of public services through Private Finance Initiatives and the disbanding of long established British regiments. And yet we all pay heavily to be members of this club. We pay in extra taxes and fees and we pay because the cost of everyday items is greater than it would be if we were not members of the EU. Since we joined the EU taxes have doubled in real terms – but the quality of our national infrastructure has collapsed.

There are many myths and misunderstandings about the EU and most of them are a result of misinformation spread by those who have a vested interest in promoting the organisation. Simple, resolutely maintained lies are incredibly difficult to break; especially if they are pronounced with dignity, confidence and certainty and supported by platoons of expensively shod individuals all saying exactly the same thing in different languages. The biggest myth of all, the lie that overshadows all other lies, is that the EU is some sort of trading partnership designed to protect our wealth and our security without affecting our national identity, our culture, our identity. This lie had been exposed many times; most recently by someone called Frau Reding, the vice president of the European Commission . Early in 2014, Frau Reding called for a `true political union' and a campaign for the European Union to become a `United States of Europe'. Hitler's dream, Hitler's words.

The EU is built on the principle of `privilege' in precisely the same way that Nazi Germany and the Soviet Union were run. The aim of the EU's supporters (and this includes all three main political parties in the UK) is to eliminate national boundaries, national governments and political parties which promote nationalism. The aim is not to produce a federation of separate states but a single State with a single management structure, a single foreign policy and a single tax system. The aim is to eliminate national armies and local police forces and to replace them with EU forces, responsible only to the EU commissioners. The aim is to eliminate all national laws and to replace them with laws devised by the EU to suit its supporters. (The EU is doing well. Around 90% of laws now being passed by the British Parliament come direct from Brussels and were devised by unelected civil servants who think up new legislation at a terrifying speed, and without, it seems, ever thinking through the consequences. The EU has so far given us around 150,000 new laws and it is still creating new laws at the rate of 3,000 a year. The House of Commons does not have a choice about whether to `pass' these laws and so British Ministers are regularly seen trying to explain new legislation to which they and their party are vehemently opposed. Directives, which come from the EU commissioners, need to be automatically placed within the national laws of each member state while `regulations', which are created by unelected and anonymous eurocrats, have the authority of laws, take immediate effect and cannot be ignored or overturned.) The plan is to eliminate electoral control by putting all important decision making processes into the hands of paid eurocrats who are controlled by the string pullers who have put themselves in charge of Hitler's dream. It was George

Orwell who pointed out that in Germany the Nazi Party controlled investment, raw materials, rates of interest, working hours and wages and it is difficult to see any difference between the control enjoyed by the Nazis and the control enjoyed by European Commissioners. The ultimate aim of the EU is not to improve the lives of ordinary people but to benefit the eurocrats. In the EU, as in Nazi Germany and the USSR, even low level staff enjoy short working hours, long holidays, huge salaries, low or no taxes, seemingly unlimited perks and privileges and an extraordinary amount of power which is used to defend and expand the EU and to protect and enrich the organisations friends and protectors (within the EU the sound of backs being scratched is sometimes quite deafening). It is always important to remember that former British Prime Minister, Edward Heath, a self-confessed liar and a traitor, was rewarded with a tax free £35,000 when he knowingly and fraudulently sold his country to the European Union (which was then masquerading under the title 'Common Market'). The sum of £35,000 may not sound much of a bribe but in today's money the bribe was worth £391,573 and we must remember that Heath was not a rich man and he had expensive hobbies.

In 1975, when discussing the forthcoming referendum on the Common Market, Heath told the British people: 'There is no question of any erosion of essential national sovereignty.' Heath said this despite the fact that the Lord Chancellor had written to him, before he signed the Treaty of Rome, saying: 'I must emphasise that in my view the surrenders of sovereignty involved are serious ones...these objections ought to be bought out into the open.' Despite the fact that he knew that joining the EU meant creating a European federal state, with monetary, political and military union an inevitability, Heath promised that joining would involve no surrender of essential sovereignty. An internal memorandum justified the deception by arguing that the British people would not notice what had happened until the end of the 20th century by which time it would be far too late to do anything about it. Just over twenty years later, in 1998, Heath was asked if he had known that joining the Common Market would lead to a federal Europe. 'Of course I bloody did,' he replied. Since then successive Prime Ministers have given away more and more of our sovereignty.

We pay huge sums of money to the EU so that unelected individuals with unlimited authority and no real responsibility or accountability can build huge, expensive offices where they can sit and think up new rules and regulations governing the way we live and what we must, and must not, do with our lives, our earnings, our savings and our property. (EU officials and their defenders like to describe their new laws as 'rules', 'directives' and 'regulations' but it seems to us that a 'rule' which authorises armed men in uniforms to take away those who break it, is entitled to be called a 'law'.) 'It is necessary,' said an EU employee recently, 'to compose a regulation to cover every area of human activity, process and production.' He didn't say why it is 'necessary' but it isn't difficult to guess. It is this deep affection for regulations and forced obedience (a real Nazi legacy) which has destroyed our commercial competitiveness, mortally damaged productivity, forced up energy prices and ensured that the EU's share of the world gross domestic product has been steadily declining for years. One of the EU's own past commissioners has admitted that EU regulations cost the European economy around £700 billion a year – outweighing by far any benefits that the single market might bring. Moreover, since other parts of the world (including the USA, China and India) have none of these nonsensical laws, Europeans are destined to become ever poorer. (Large multinational companies love the high regulation environment of the EU because their lobbying ensures that the regulations which are created are designed to crush small companies which might turn out to be competitors.)

The truth is that the people who designed and created the EU, and the hubristic, strutting eurocrats who now run it, have succeeded in manufacturing an organisation which is both Statist and Fascist in nature. It is important to remember this because the EU's defenders and supporters invariably dismiss the organisation's critics as `fascists' and yet the truth is that the EU itself fits the fascist ideal more closely than any other organisation in history.

A look at the dictionary helps to establish the truth about the EU.

The Oxford Dictionary of English defines statism as: `a political system in which the State has substantial centralised control over social and economic affairs'. We would be surprised if a better definition of the European Union than that exists. It is important to remember that statism has been tried, tested extensively and for long periods and proved to do nothing to enrich or empower ordinary working folk but everything to empower the State, in the person of the bureaucrats and their cronies.

But then there is `fascism'. The same dictionary defines fascism as `an authoritarian and nationalistic right wing system of government and social organisation' and adds that there must also be a contempt for democracy and a `strong insistence' on obedience to the leadership. Once again, that fits the EU perfectly. The EU is both statist and fascist. It is often conveniently forgotten but Oswald Mosley, Britain's leading fascist in the 1930s, was a firm supporter of Hitler's plan for a European Union.

The EU might not yet have official status as a nation but it has its own flag, anthem, police force, diplomats and parliament and there is absolutely no doubt that the people who support and defend the EU regard it as having a sort of nation status. Baroness Ashton, the superstate's first Foreign Secretary (known both officially and by aficionados of the operas of W.S.Gilbert and Sir Arthur Sullivan as the High Representative), recently found time in her busy schedule to demand her own EU army. All we now need is an official Walther Funk Day to celebrate the EU's founder.

The big, unasked, question is, of course, what is the EU for? Who really benefits?

And the answer, of course, is Germany. It is no coincidence that just about every country in the European Union is getting poorer while Germany continues to get richer and richer.

We may think we won the Second World War.
But we lost.

It is no surprise that we are all living in a foreign country: we are now living in the Fourth Reich. Knowingly or not those who support and defend the European Union are supporting the Nazi legacy.

Incidentally, much of the information in this book will probably be new to you. Politicians are, for a variety of reasons, often unwilling to tell the truth about the European Union. Some are silent because they are afraid of the consequences of speaking out. Others keep quiet because they have been bribed by the EU.

Part Two: The EU Was Inspired and Designed by Nazis

Those who support the EU claim that it is a modern creation which was devised after World War II to ensure that Europe would never again be ripped apart by war. There are enthusiastic supporters who claim that the EU was founded by Kohl and Mitterand. We have heard it suggested on the BBC (an organisation known to support and defend the EU) that these two politicians were so scarred by their memories of World War II that they decided to build a new Europe `where there would be peace, happiness and prosperity for all'.

This is a fairy tale of such Brobdingnagian proportions that even the Grimm Brothers and Baron von Munchausen would have blushed with embarrassment. And yet there are many credulous citizens who believe it.

The truth is that the history of the EU goes back much, much further than its proponents will usually admit.

It was back in the 1930's, in Hitler's Germany, that the European Union was invented and designed. Hitler wanted to destroy national identities and create a united Europe, consisting of new regions to be ruled from Berlin. `In 1936 Hitler told the Reichstag: `It is not very intelligent to imagine that in such a cramped house like that of Europe, a community of peoples can maintain different legal systems and different concepts of law for long.' Even before that, in Italy, the founding father of fascism, Mussolini, said in 1933 that: `Europe may once again grasp the helm of world civilisation if it can develop a modicum of political unity.'

Hitler was the man who gave bones to the dreams first expressed by Charlemagne and Napoleon but the finishing touches to the EU as we know it were put in place during World War II by a man called Walther Funk, who was President of the Reichsbank and a director of the Bank for International Settlements (BIS). It was Funk who predicted the coming of European economic unity. Funk was also Adolf Hitler's economics minister and his key economics advisor.

The European Union was designed by Nazis and it has been carefully created according to the original design. It is not, you will note, a `group' or an `association'. It was always a union. And in a union the members are not affiliated, they are joined. `What good fortune for governments that the people do not think,' said Adolf Hitler.

The BIS, by the way, was then and still is the world's most powerful and secret global financial institution. During the Second World War the BIS accepted looted Nazi gold (handling 21.5 metric tons of Nazi gold) and supported the development and launch of what would, in 2002, become the euro.

The EU's fans like to pretend that the fine points of the organisation were planned in the 1980's and 1990's. But it was Hitler and Funk who designed the EU as it exists today. The Nazis wanted to get rid of the clutter of small nations which made up Europe and their plan was quite simple. The EU was Hitler's dream. And it was Funk who outlined the practical work which needed to be done.

In 1940, Funk prepared a lengthy memo called `Economic Reorganisation of Europe' which was passed to the President of the BIS (who was an American called Thomas McKittrick) on July 26th 1940.

`The new European economy will result from close economic collaboration between German and European countries,' wrote Funk. It is important to note that even then the EU was seen as a union between Germany, on the one hand, and the rest of Europe, on the other. There was never any doubt which nation would be in charge of the new United States of Europe. (The phrase United States of Europe was devised by Adolf Hitler himself). There are commentators and economists today who note Germany's control of today's EU with surprise, and who seem puzzled by the fact that Germany is booming and has by far the largest and most dominant economy in the EU. No one should be surprised because the EU was always planned that way. Germany is benefitting enormously from the euro crisis but Funk knew that would be the case. Back in 1940, Funk had the idea for the euro but warned that even after monetary union it would be impossible to have one standard of living throughout Europe. He knew that the euro would be flawed but he also he knew that Germany would come out on top. He would not be in the slightest bit surprised by the fact that modern Germany is by far the largest and most dominant economy in the European Union. That was always the Plan. In reality, of course, the euro was bound to cause chaos and massive unemployment throughout many parts of the European Union because of policies which German politicians set in process after the unification of West and East Germany and before the foundation of the euro. The policies, which were designed to enable a unified Germany to control the EU, involved Germany entering the euro at an advantageously low exchange rate, thereby giving it a huge competitive advantage over other euro countries. The aim was that Germany would get richer while other countries got poorer and that is exactly what is happening. (The French chose to join the euro with a strong franc because it meant that they could enjoy cheap holidays in the rest of Europe.) The result is that because the euro is undervalued relative to the German economy, Germany exports far more than it imports and grows ever richer and stronger at the expense of its other euro `partners'. The fact is that Germany currently runs the world's biggest trade surplus – and has been running big surpluses for a decade. German politicians have refused to spend the money they have been accumulating and so other countries in Europe, struggling to cope with a euro artificially strengthened by a rich Germany, have slumped further and further into depression and their unemployment rates have soared.

The Germans are fighting hard to protect and preserve the euro, and will continue to pay money to preserve the status quo, because if the European currency breaks up two things will happen: first, Hitler's plan for a German dominated United States of Europe will be in tatters and second, the Germany mark will be as strong as the Swiss franc, and cars and refrigerators made in Germany will be priced out of many markets. If the Germans can keep the euro alive then in due course, the inevitable will happen: Germany will control the European Union and Hitler will have a posthumous victory. Economists, who tend to have a limited understanding of the world, are constantly producing articles expressing surprise at the fact that the euro was created at all and dismay that, despite all the evidence showing that it has caused enormous damage to countries and individuals, it is being kept alive. If they understood how and why the European Union was created (and who created it) they would, perhaps, have a better understanding of why it exists and why those who support it will fight to the death to preserve it. The europhiles know well that if the euro disappears the EU will be mortally wounded and that no one will ever again dare to try recreating it: the Nazi dream will be lost for ever.

Remember all this the next time you see a British politician claiming that our enormously expensive membership of the EU is vital for Britain. And remember too that many of the EU's loudest and most persistent supporters have received massive financial support from the EU; sometimes in the form of grants and sometimes as fees. The EU spends billions every year on keeping its supporters happy. The BBC, a renowned supporter of the European Union and an organisation which has confessed to being biased in the EU's favour, has received millions of pounds from the EU. The money is invariably described as being given as a `grant' but the word `bribe' might be more appropriate. The BBC seems to repay this financial support by defending unpopular EU policies (such as those on immigration), by insisting that all measurements referred to in its programmes are in EU friendly metric units rather than proper British imperial measurements and by taking every opportunity to disparage England and the English. Joseph Goebbels, the Minister of Propaganda in the Third Reich, would have been proud of the BBC which is now an essential part of the Fourth Reich. He would have probably also been proud of the fact that scores of universities have professors funded by the EU. The professors are paid to teach students the value of European integration. And, naturally, the EU has, over the years, spent many large fortunes producing literature and teaching aids for teachers to use in European schools. On the rare occasions when voters in European countries have been invited to vote on EU issues the EU has been the main contributor to `Vote Yes' campaigns. In 1975, when Britons were last given the opportunity to air their views on the EU, the EU helped fund the `Vote Yes' campaign.

In 1941, Walther Funk was still planning the new European Union. He launched the Europaische Wirtschafts Gemeinschaft (European Economic Community) to integrate the European economy into a single market and to establish his idea for a single European currency. It was Funk who helped plan the European Union Community although when it was established he was still labelled a war criminal and still a resident of Spandau Prison in Berlin and it wasn't considered a terribly good idea to give him medals or to organise a thank you `roast'. All subsequent suggestions that Funk be recognised as the founding father of the European Union have been rejected on the grounds that it is too soon to put up a statue to the man to whom Hitler handed the responsibility of ensuring the good health of the Fourth Reich. Funk thought up everything and planned the EU in precise detail. It was even Funk who planned a Europe free of trade and currency restrictions. In June 1942, German officials prepared a document entitled `Basic Elements of a Plan for the New Europe' which called, among other things, for a European clearing centre to stabilise currency rates with the aim of securing European monetary union and `the harmonisation of labour conditions and social welfare'.

The original plan was for the Reichsmark to be the new European currency but Funk never saw this as crucial, or being as important as Germany having economic leadership of Europe. The far-sighted Funk saw Germany as central to the planned EU, and argued that it would result in `better outlets for German goods on European markets'. Back in 1940 it was Funk who planned to introduce a United States of Europe via a common currency. Today, it is clear that Walther Funk, economist, banker and war criminal, is the true father of the modern European Union and is one of the most influential figures in European history.

Hitler and the rest of the Nazi leadership welcomed Funk's plans and in 1942 the German Foreign Ministry made detailed plans for a European confederation to be dominated by Germany. In the same year a group of German businessmen held a conference in Berlin entitled `European Economic Community'. (The phrase `European Economic Community had been first used by Hermann Goerring in 1940.) In 1942, Reinhard Heydrich, who was head of the Reich Security Central Office and renowned for his ruthlessness against enemies of the State, published `The Reich Plan for the Domination of Europe' – a document which is notable for its remarkable similarity to the EU's Treaty of Rome. In March 1943, 13 countries (including France and Italy) were invited to join a new European federation which would be under German military control.

When the Nazis realised that they were losing the war they knew that they had to make a deal in order to preserve German domination in Europe. Thomas McKittrick, the president of the BIS, acted as go between and helped set up the negotiations. The underlying plan was to ensure that Germany dominated post-war Europe and Funk and his colleagues decided to talk about European spirit, liberty, equality, fraternity and worldwide cooperation as the basis for their planned European Union. They decided to agree to share power, and even to allow other countries to take charge for a while. The Nazis knew that all they needed to do was retain men in power in crucial posts. And this they succeeded in doing. In 1944 a secret conference was held in Berlin entitled `How Will Germany Dominate The Peace When It Loses The War'. Rich and powerful Germans decided to move a huge amount of money out of Germany and to take it to America. (The money stayed there until after the Nurnberg Trials when it came back to Europe.) In August 1944, the heads of the Nazi Government and a group of leading German industrialists, met at a hotel in Strasbourg and decided to hide more large sums of money in order to pay for the fight for a German dominated Europe to continue if their country lost the war. The Nazis realised that their back-up plan for European domination would take years to reach fruition but they believed that if their military tactics failed then their subtle economic and political tactics would prove successful. Today, of course, Strasbourg is the seat of the Council of Europe and the European Parliament although maybe to avoid the embarrassment of being headquartered exclusively in a town the Nazis favoured, the EU moves documents and people to Brussels once a month. The whole pointless operation costs over £100 million a year and must cause enormous inconvenience and delay. What an amazing coincidence it is that such a small and otherwise insignificant town should have been both the site of such an important Nazi meeting and the home for the European Union. (Strasbourg was captured by Germany during the Franco-German War in 1870 but was handed back to France after World War I. It was occupied by Germany and the Nazis during World War II but became French again after that war.)

The technical preparations for Funk's `European Large Unit Economy' (now better known as the Eurozone) began in 1947 when the Paris accord on multilateral payments was signed, were strengthened in 1951 when the European Coal and Steel Community was created as the first step towards the development of a new European nation to be run by Germany, and continued in 1964 when the Committee of European Central Banks (made up of Bank Governors) met at the BIS to coordinate monetary policy. In 1961 President Kennedy told British Prime Minister Harold Macmillan that the White House would only support Britain's application to join the Common Market if Britain accepted that the true goal of the Common Market was political integration – Hitler's famous United States of Europe. In 1966, American President Johnson encouraged Britain's membership of the developing European Economic Community and so Foreign Office civil servants in London decided that the `special relationship' with the USA would be enhanced if Britain joined the Common Market. In 1968, the Foreign Office warned that `if we fail to become part of a more united Europe, Britain's links with the USA will not be enough to prevent us becoming increasingly peripheral to USA concerns'.

The European Central Bank (ECB), (which today has so much power over European citizens) was designed and set up by the German Bundesbank which was Germany's post war central bank. The Bundesbank was the son of the Reichsbank which was the name of Germany's central bank before and during World War II. The President of the Reichsbank before and during World War II was, of course, Walther Funk. The ECB would probably have a Walther Funk Founder's Day if they thought they could get away with it and the only surprise that Funk hasn't yet found himself portrayed on euro coins and notes. He has more of a right to appear on them than anyone else because they were his idea.

Today, thanks to the Maastricht Treaty, each EU member's gold reserves belong to the EU and are effectively controlled by the ECB. As planned, the ECB (grandson of Hitler's Reichsbank) is not democratically accountable to anyone. It is actually prohibited from taking advice from Eurozone Governments and the European Parliament has no authority over it. No one knows how the ECB makes decisions because everything is done in great secrecy.

There are some supporters of the EU who claim that the absence of democracy within the organisation was never the original attention. They are wrong. The EU was always designed to be an undemocratic organisation: it is the Anti-Democracy. Way back in 1950, Clement Attlee, Britain's Labour Prime Minister recognised the problems associated with the planned European unity. He said, when responding to the Schuman plan for the European Coal and Steel Community (the initial version of the EU): `It (is) impossible for Britain to accept the principle that the economic forces of this country should be handed over to an authority that is utterly undemocratic and is responsible to nobody.'

The unwritten, unspoken aims of the European Union are to regulate every activity and to ensure that everything which every citizen does will be controlled by the State. The plan is to eliminate small businesses, small hospitals and small everything else. As far as the EU is concerned `small is bad'. It is much easier for the State to control production and tax gathering if it only has to deal with large international companies. (It is hardly surprising that the executives of large companies are among the most vocal of the EU's supporters. In the UK, for example, they will often threaten to close down factories if citizens vote to leave the EU.) By licensing every occupation, and insisting that individuals pay annual licensing fees, the EU can control citizens and take in more taxes. Individuals who speak out or protest can be controlled by having their licenses withdrawn.

On January 1ˢᵗ 1999, eleven countries launched the euro and in January 2002 Funk's dream currency finally replaced national currencies. The secretive BIS was crucial in helping to force through the euro – the first step towards the new European state. The truth is that the introduction of the euro was nothing more than the final instalment of World War II – the realisation of the Nazi dream shared by Adolf Hitler and Walther Funk. Herr Funk had predicted that uniting countries with different cultures and economic policies would be disastrous. But he knew Germany would come out on top.

Members of the British press were massively enthusiastic about the euro but got so excited that they forgot to give due credit to Herr Funk and his boss. Commentators drew attention to the fact that travellers could now use the same currency over much of Europe and could buy ice creams in Italy with money they'd taken out of the bank in France. No attention was paid to the fact that when countries decide to share a currency they are making a significant political decision. No one seemed to care that the majority of people in all the countries which gave up their currencies were opposed to the euro. (The EU has never pretended to be a democratic organisation. Hitler and Funk believed in federalism and centralisation but they weren't desperately enthusiastic about democracy which they regarded as a sign of weak leadership.)

`It was a very peculiar thing to have a central bank without a Government,' said Paul Volcker, chairman of the Federal Reserve in the USA. French politicians believed that the single currency meant that Germany would not be able to start any more wars. They also believed (quite wrongly, of course) that Germany would no longer be able to dominate the European economy.

Everyone involved with the creation of the euro knew that the new currency was fatally flawed. The aim was to use the euro to force through a political union, against the will of the European people and in spite of the massive, inevitable cost in terms of unemployment and hardship. Millions of people now face a lifetime of poverty and unemployment because of the hasty introduction of a new currency which no one needed and no one wanted.

Economists recognised from the start that the euro would be problematic and would create huge social difficulties (including terrible levels of unemployment) but politicians ignored all the warnings. They knew that introducing the euro would make the creation of a federal Europe inevitable and unstoppable.

In 1945, Hitler's Masterplan was captured by the Allies. The Plan included details of his scheme to create an economic integration of Europe and to found a European Union on a federal basis. The Nazi plan for a federal Europe was based on Lenin's belief that `federation is a transitional form towards complete union of all nations'.

It is impossible to find any difference between Hitler's plan for a new United States of Europe, dominated by Germany, and the European Union we have today.

The whole EU project was built on dishonesty. It was never wanted by the people of Europe and it has been built on years of deceit, corruption and hidden agendas. A group of fanatics, inspired by Hitler's dream of a United States of Europe, realised that their dream could only be turned into reality if they moved one small step at a time, set limited objectives, ignored public opinion and prepared treaties which required individual countries to relinquish only a little of their sovereignty in any one agreement. And so a relatively innocuous Coal and Steel Community was slowly transformed into the European Union – soon to be the United States of Europe.

Part Three: 73 Things You Ought to Know About the EU (Facts the BBC Forgot to Tell You)

There is considerable confusion about which laws originated with the EU. This is not an accident. Politicians have been told that they must not `blame' the EU for unpopular legislation. Most politicians in power are happy to obey this ruling partly because they do not want to appear to be acting as mere puppets, dancing to the string pullers in Brussels and Strasbourg, and partly because they do not want to find themselves excluded when the `thank you' goodies (jobs, grants, fees etc) are being distributed. And the EU has proved extremely adept at spinning the truth about its own powers. It's important to remember that the EU spends over £2 billion a year on advertising itself. That's more than Coca Cola spends on advertising and it buys an awful lot of loyalty from media groups.

We have prepared a list of just some of the ways in which EU legislation has affected the way we live. This list is not comprehensive, of course. It is not unreasonable to assume that any new legislation which seems incomprehensible or which has made life worse in any way will have originated with the EU.

1.

Immigration Is Impoverishing Britain
The EU insists on a free flow of migrants between countries not to give people freedom but because Hitler's basic aim was to create a new, single nation which would appear to be an independent nation state but which would, in practice, be ruled by Germany. Hitler and Funk realised that immigration into countries such as England would reduce any sense of patriotism or nationalism. People who move into a country rarely care as much about that country's culture or mores as those who were born there and this is particularly true if the immigrants are inspired simply by the prospect of free money. As a side issue they also realised that allowing people to move around helps industry because it ensures that cheap labour can be found where it is needed most. And a truly fascist state, such as the European Union, must, of course, cater to the needs of large industries.

The British Government argues that immigration is necessary in order to counteract the cost of an ageing nation. The Government says that we need immigrants to boost our work force. This is arrant nonsense, of course. It is jobs not workers that we need. We already have lots of potential employees but the problem is that many don't want to work and don't see why they should work when it is easier and more profitable to use the benefits system to their advantage. The British theory is that because most of the immigrants will be Muslim, and most Muslim couples have large families, the average age of the nation will be reduced and there will be plenty of young Muslim workers available to work, pay tax and pay the cost of the nation's pension commitments. The naïve assumption, which we are expected to accept, is that Muslim workers, who have no allegiance to Britain, and may hate us for our military adventures, political policies and support of Israel, will be keen to pay the pensions of millions of retired Christians. All this is disingenuous nonsense, designed to provide an explanation for the Government's craven acceptance of the deeply unpopular immigration rules imposed on by the EU's eurocrats. Anyone who questions the rationale, and who wonders how such a small island can cope with such a rapidly growing population is dismissed as a racist and silenced by embarrassment or arrest.

Naturally, all this ignores the fact that the real reason for the EU's immigration policy is that Hitler realised that the easiest and quickest way to break down traditional geographical barriers, and to destroy varieties of nationalism and patriotism which are not Teutonic in nature, is to encourage people to move countries without accepting their new country's culture.

Any politician who had the courage to reject the EU's bribes, grants, fees and promises and to tell immigrants to accept our way of life or to go back whence they came would (if they managed to avoid arrest on some charge created by the politically-correct friends of the EU) find themselves enjoying a landslide victory of unprecedented proportions. Instead, our politicians tell British electors that they must accept whatever changes the immigrants demand, that they must abandon their culture, forget their history and adapt their laws and social habits to avoid offending the incomers. All this is, of course, designed to destroy the will of the English and to ensure that everything English is regarded as embarrassingly racist and consigned to the EU-approved wheelie bin.

The UK's bizarre and unique gold plating of the EU's immigration policies (by providing financial benefits and free homes for immigrants) has encouraged most poor Europeans to head for England, impoverishing the nation and putting an insupportable strain on the country's infrastructure. The British Government recently admitted that in a single year 2,600,000 foreigners had applied to stay in Britain. It is no wonder that our small island feels crowded and that our infrastructure is creaking badly. Many immigrants prefer to send most of the free money back home and to live as cheaply as they can while in England; they travel to England not because they are keen to visit Shakespeare's birthplace, the Tower of London and Buckingham Palace but because they are attracted by our benefits system, our child support system, our jobseekers' allowances and our National Health Service. They are not interested in our culture, and expect to be allowed to preserve their own cultural rules while living in England. (Most immigrants stay in England. Not many bother to journey as far as Scotland, Wales or Northern Ireland because it's quicker and cheaper to get back home if you stay in England.) Very few immigrants take any interest in the history, culture or mores of the country which is feeding them and, indeed, our Government does not expect them to do so.

Immigrants who want to become British must be able to show that they know their rights as EU citizens, how to obtain legal aid, how to claim unemployment benefits, how to use legislation designed to outlaw discrimination, how to complain about sexual harassment, how to seek compensation for unfair dismissal and details of the minimum wage and holiday pay. They must have a working knowledge of how the EU operates. There is, however, no need for them to know anything much about British history or culture. Most immigrants don't even bother to learn the English language – with the result that one in five children living in England now speaks little or no English. (It's no wonder that the incidence of illiteracy in Britain is rising at such a pace). Vast numbers of immigrants simply demand that Britain provide them with help and information in their own language and the EU forces Britain to employ expensive teams of lawyers and translators to help them. The National Health Service (NHS) alone spends £55 million on translators. The attractions of a life in Britain are clear to see and it is not surprising that since 2003 well over two million foreign nationals have obtained British National Insurance numbers and are entitled to benefits paid by long-suffering British taxpayers. This really ought to worry us. Over 500 million citizens of the EU are entitled to claim unemployment benefits, child benefits and the cornucopia of financial goodies which Britain alone offers; all they have to do is to jump on a bus, a train or a plane and head for the UK.

And so, as the EU migrants pour into Britain, our roundabouts are dotted with `temporary' camp sites; scruffy, insanitary shanty towns are turning up on bits of waste land everywhere and thousands of immigrants are living in sheds, or crammed 12 to a room in conditions that would have appalled Charles Dickens. Muslim vigilantes patrol city streets and terrorise couples who dare hold hands and ancient universities put male and female students in separate lecture rooms in order to satisfy the demands of Islamic lecturers. No wonder even the immigrants who have been here a year or two would like to see immigration stopped.

The politicians who excuse these developments (in deference to the wishes of the eurocrats) are, of course, protected from the consequences of immigration ; official homes, chauffeur-driven cars and police protection ensure that they never have to come face to face with reality. They can always turn their heads and sniff a cologne-soaked handkerchief if their chauffeur takes a wrong turning and takes them past a bunch of Roma immigrants defaecating in a gutter.

Hitler, Funk and Mussolini would have been delighted by the way things are working out. If they'd had half a sense of humour between them they would have been chortling with glee. Things could not have worked out better for the Fourth Reich.

British politicians have almost always underestimated the impact of EU immigration policies. A decade ago, when Polish citizens were given unlimited freedom to move to the UK, Government ministers officially estimated that a modest 13,000 Poles would move to Britain. It wouldn't be 12,000 or 14,000 but it would be 13,000. They never explained how they managed to produce such a curiously precise figure but in the end that didn't really matter because their estimate was out by around 987,000. The EU has now given Romanians and Bulgarians carte blanche to travel to Britain (and has forbidden the British Government the right to refuse to pay them cash benefits when they arrive). Politicians were there at the airport to meet and welcome the first new bunch of migrants in January 2014.

The truth is that since Heath, Thatcher, Major, Blair and Brown signed away our heritage, our politicians have had no more control over immigration than anyone else. Even if they want to do something, our current weedy crew of `leaders' (Cameron, Clegg and Miliband) have no power to stop the immigrants or to prevent them having the same rights as British taxpayers. They may pretend they have. But they know they haven't. We are none of us British now; as it says on the front of our passports these days, we are all citizens of the European Union. The bit about the United Kingdom is there to appease the sceptics and will soon be quietly removed. Politicians may talk of clamp downs and limits and restrictions on paying out cash to immigrants but they have no power to introduce any of these things.

Politicians in other countries may ignore the orders from the Fourth Reich but politicians in Britain gold plate them. (The phrase `gold plating' refers to the habit of over-implementing new laws passed by the EU.) Many British politicians have been `bought' by the European Union and are, in consequence, constantly looking for new lies to tell in support of the organisation. Although the EU is a Nazi invention most of its supporters are not Nazis; they are either dupes who misunderstand the purpose of the organisation or they are politicians, corporate executives and cheap grafters bought and paid for with grants, fees and deals.

The consequence of the EU's forced immigration policy is that in October 2013 an EU study found that 611,779 unemployed immigrants (and their families) were living in Britain and claiming full benefits. The Government was unable to work out just how much this was costing British taxpayers but estimated that the unemployed immigrants were costing the NHS alone at least £1.5 billion a year. As a result of the number of foreigners coming into England because of the free money on offer (just why our politicians express surprise that impoverished foreigners should choose to come here to accept the free money we want to give them is one the great mysteries of life) our population is rising faster than anywhere else in Europe. Our island has been overcrowded for decades but parts of it are now becoming unbearably so. And every aspect of our way of life has been damaged irretrievably. Over half of black children live in one parent homes (it is, not surprisingly perhaps, usually the father who is missing). Largely as a result of forced marriages, one third of Pakistani mothers in parts of Northern England are related to the father of their children (with the result that the incidence of mental infirmity is rocketing). Young white girls are abused by Asian gangs. There are parts of our country where the consumption of alcohol is not allowed because local Muslims disapprove. (I'd like to see what happened if a group of English boozers insisted on defying the law and opening a pub in Riyadh.)

As if all that were not bad enough, things will soon get considerably worse. Now that the citizens of Romania and Bulgaria are allowed free access to Britain (and to Britain's nanny state, over-generous infrastructure and benefits system) the chances are high that the number of immigrants in an already overcrowded country will rocket still higher. And those who claim that this influx of immigrants will make the country richer are being disingenuous at best because EU laws allow workers who have jobs abroad to pay taxes in their own countries. So, any Romanians, Bulgarians and others who do choose to work in Britain will be able to pay taxes in Romania (where tax rates are lower) and send their savings home to their relatives. Britain will pay out billions but receive nothing in return. At the end of 2013 the Government estimated that 100,000 immigrants in Britain were already taking advantage of this legitimate form of EU-approved tax evasion.

And when the eurocrats aren't thinking up ways to make things worse there are plenty of others prepared to do their work for them. In December 2013 it was announced that the Maltese were planning to sell EU passports for 650,000 euros each, allowing those buying the passports to take up immediate residence in other EU countries, including Britain. Naturally, the Maltese said that they would only sell passports to honest, decent folk with impeccable reputations. I'm sure they are right (though we cannot immediately explain to ourselves why honest, decent folk with impeccable reputations would want to buy a passport) but it does seem quite likely that other governments within the EU might see this as an irresistible commercial opportunity.

To be fair, it is perhaps only reasonable to point out that other countries within the EU also sell passports to people who are regarded as rich enough to deserve them. And it may well be that British politicians and civil servants who criticised the Maltese plan were miffed because the

Mediterranean country was planning to see citizenship at a lower price than the UK which runs a bizarre means-testing scheme whereby those applying for permanent residence must invest £1 million, £5 million or £10 million in shares or gilts in order to be granted permission to apply for permanent residence in five, three or two years respectively.

2.
The EU Promotes Corporate Tax Dodging

One of the basic principles of fascism is that big companies must be protected in every possible way. It is, for example, to protect large companies that the EU constantly produces new rules and regulations. Most of these oppressive new laws (referred to, rather lightly, as `red tape') are created by lobbyists and political advisers working for big companies. The lobbyists and advisers have specific agendas to promote. (Estimates suggest that there are around 20,000 lobbyists living and working in Brussels. MEPs have boasted of having earned hundreds of thousands of euros for introducing amendments to EU legislation. There is good evidence showing that the companies which spend the most on lobbyists are the most profitable.) The eurocrats simply turn the corporate proposals into legislation. Small companies are strangled by the red tape but big companies simply create new departments to deal with the bureaucratic consequences. Moreover, the founding treaty of the European Union gives companies the right to move their income to the country where they want to pay tax rather than the country where the income is earned. (It does not, of course, give individuals the opportunity to earn their money in the United Kingdom and to not pay tax on it in Monaco.) The money doesn't even have to stay within the EU. The Maastricht Treaty of 1992 gave companies the right to pay their corporate taxes outside the boundaries of the European Union if they could find more amenable tax havens elsewhere. All the company has to do is to establish a head office in a tax free zone. British politicians can complain about large companies avoiding their tax liabilities but they cannot do a thing about it.

3.
The EU Has Given Itself the Right to Confiscate Your Savings

The EU aims to have control of all the taxes collected within constituent countries. Customs duties collected at British ports already go directly to the EU. In addition the EU collects a percentage of our VAT revenue and a percentage of our total Gross Domestic Product. Britain has always been a net contributor to the EU. Other EU countries, including France and Germany, often receive vast amounts of money in grants and special payments. The EU now has the right to collect taxes (even if they are not always described as taxes) in any way it sees fit. For example, in April 2013 unelected eurocrats put a special tax on savers who had deposited money in banks on the island of Cyprus. The aim was to enable the EU to take money from ordinary citizens in order to protect the EU and big banks from losses. It is widely expected that the EU will soon introduce special wealth and property taxes on savers and home owners in Britain.

4.
The EU Opposes Nationalism But Supports Scottish Independence

It may seem odd to some that the EU should support Scottish independence. It is, after all, well known that the EU's supporters are firmly opposed to any form of nationalism. When England won the rugby World Cup a few years ago politicians described the success as a `win for Europe'. But there is a good reason for this apparent anomaly.

Those who support the idea of an independent Scotland mistakenly believe that the EU is on their side and that by helping to support the Scottish Parliament the EU has endorsed the hopes and ideals of flag waving, kilt wearing Scots. The Scottish nationalists have, of course, completely misunderstood the way the EU works, and the reason for the existence of a Scottish Parliament. Scotland is already an EU region. If the Scots vote to leave the UK, Scotland will still be an EU region. The EU will support Scottish independence, which it sees as an aid in breaking up the UK.

5.

The EU Plans to Break the UK Into a Series of Regions

The EU has always planned to divide the UK up into a series of regions – with each region having a regional parliament.

The Scottish Parliament, the Northern Ireland Assembly, the Welsh Parliament and the London Assembly are all nothing more than regional parliaments designed to ensure that new laws from Brussels are passed on to the local peasantry. (The London Assembly is the EU's regional parliament for the London area of England.) The original idea was quite brilliant. The plan was to trick locals into thinking that they were being given real control over what happened in their area. The EU has built itself up by bribing, bullying terrorising and tricking the electorates of European countries and in some parts of the UK the idea of tricking citizens into thinking that they were being given more, rather than less, autonomy has worked extremely well. There are millions of people who believe that these so-called parliaments were designed to give independence to those regions. They're wrong, of course. These fake parliaments were authorised in order to help break up the United Kingdom. It was announced that there were plans for other so-called elected parliaments in the officially designated nine regions of England, and the Labour Government organised a referendum in the North East of England (where it was thought the idea would be most likely to receive support) to ask the people there if they would like a Regional Assembly. Despite the spending of a huge amount of public money on a campaign for a `yes' vote the people voted overwhelmingly to reject the idea. It was a humiliating defeat for the Labour Party in general and for John Prescott who had spearheaded the campaign. It was not a defeat for the EU because the EU was never mentioned during the campaign and very few people realised that the whole idea was part of the EU's plan for the regionalisation of England. Despite this defeat (which took place in 2004 and, rather appropriately, on November 5th) the North Eastern Regional Parliament – the one the people of the North East said they didn't want – was actually alive and financially very well. The Parliament (or Assembly) was already in existence when the people of the North East were invited to say whether or not they should exist. Moreover, there were seven other unelected regional parliaments in other parts of England. (The word 'unelected' appears regularly in any document referring to the European Union. The EU is governed and run by a group of people who appoint one another, are unaccountable to the people paying their salaries, pensions and expenses, cannot be sacked and are above the law.)

The eight Regional Assemblies which the English didn't want were already set up and had buildings, staff, huge budgets and real power. They operated in secrecy because the members of these Assemblies were appointed and not elected. The Assemblies replaced the planning function of county councils and acted as regional planning bodies. The Labour Party gave them complete authority over housing and planning strategies. Decisions made by the Regional Assemblies could not be questioned or overturned. They reported direct to Brussels.

After their existence was exposed the Regional Assemblies were quietly disassembled and their powers handed to other bodies. But it is important to understand that the Regional Assemblies were established under the Regional Development Agencies Act 1998 which was a result of the 1992 Maastricht Treaty which adopted the EU regionalisation plan. The plan still exists and will abolish England's 48 counties and replace them with nine European regions. The regional parliaments will return.

The EU's plan to get rid of England and all things English has been supported by recent British Governments. Official forms often allow citizens to describe themselves as Scottish, Welsh, Irish and so on but never allow them to describe themselves as English. English councils frequently insist that the cross of St George be removed from private buildings on the grounds that it is racist to display the English flag. Schoolchildren have been sent home for wearing clothing containing the cross of St George. The BBC deemed 'The Last Night of the Proms' to be dangerously English and ordered that it be made more 'inclusive'. The Encyclopaedia Britannica reports that: 'Despite the political, economic and cultural legacy that has perpetuated its name...England no longer officially exists as a country.')

The EU also plans to erase all national borders within Europe by creating a number of new European super regions. For example, EU maps show a new region called the Arc Manche which consists of parts of Northern France and Southern England (including London). The first meeting of the Arc Manche transnational region took place in Sussex in 2006 and was chaired by a Frenchman who is the appointed President of the Region. Western England will be grouped with parts of France, Spain and Portugal to form the Atlantic Region. There are other super regions too and the EU has demanded that maps within member states be brought in line with the EU's specifications. The internet makes it fairly easy for sceptical readers to check the existence of the Arc Manche and other transnational regions.

6.
EU Energy Policies are Pushing up Prices; Putting Us at Risk of Blackouts and Causing Starvation and Death In Developing Countries

The EU has decreed that a fixed percentage of all energy used in Britain must come from 'green' sources by 2020. And it has stated that 5.75% of the transport fuel we use must be biofuel. They insist too that we generate much of our electricity from renewable sources.

These absurd and arbitrary laws have caused enormous problems and there is no doubt that they will cause even bigger problems in the future. The insistence on using biofuel for cars and lorries is particularly irrational. To reach the EU target, around 25% of all arable land in the EU region will have to be turned over to producing ethanol. Farmers who used to grow wheat and barley now grow rapeseed so that they can profit from the EU's laws. In order to find enough food the EU is now importing food from nations which desperately need the food themselves. In Swaziland, where nearly half the inhabitants are dying of starvation, agricultural land is being used to grow biofuels so that the EU's thirst for them can be satisfied. The EU's affection for biofuels means that food prices are rising and people in Africa are dying of starvation. (It is estimated that in Britain the EU's biofuel policy will add £750 to the average food bill.)

We wonder how many people working for the EU know that rapeseed oil produces lots of nitrous oxide gas, which creates even more global warming than carbon dioxide. We wonder how many know that ethanol cannot be sent along usual oil pipelines because it is corrosive and picks up impurities. We wonder how many know that this means that special tanks have to be built so that the stuff can be moved around on special trains. We wonder how many know that producing ethanol actually costs energy? (In other words we are using up more energy in producing ethanol than we obtain when we use the ethanol to fuel machinery.) And we wonder how many know that the pollution from biofuels causes serious health hazards? Ethanol burning cars increase the level of toxic ozone gas – a substance so toxic that it can crack rubber and destroy stone statues – and produce a variety of carcinogens.

Apart from being directly responsible for thousands of deaths in Africa, the EU energy policy is pushing up energy prices and will result in severe power shortages in Britain. The lights will go out and the heating will go off.

In addition, in order to comply with EU legislation, Britain has had to shut down two thirds of her coal fired operating plants. Thanks to the EU the future is bleak, dark and cold.

7.The EU Has Forced Us to Use Light Bulbs Which are More Dangerous and More Expensive than the Old Ones

The EU has forced us to replace our old, traditional, incandescent light bulbs and replace them with compact fluorescent bulbs on the grounds that the new bulbs use less energy than the old ones. The immediate cost of converting our light bulbs and lamp holders was estimated by the British Government to be around £3 billion.

The first problem with the new EU light-bulbs is that the light produced by them is so poor that people have difficulty seeing where they are going – let alone being able to see well enough to read or work. It seems clear that the new bulbs will result in far more accidents. The second problem is that the new bulbs must be kept switched on for longer than the old ones. This means using up more energy. Third, the EU-approved bulbs are bigger and heavier than the old ones and so cost more to store and transport. Fourth, the new bulbs cost up to 20 times as much as the old ones and do not always last much longer. Fifth, the EU bulbs tend to flicker and produce a harsher, less relaxing light than the bulbs the EU has banned. It seems certain that the new bulbs will cause migraines, dizziness and possibly fits. Sixth, the new bulbs cannot be used with dimmer switches or electronically triggered security lights. Millions of pounds worth of equipment will have to be replaced. Indeed, less than half of all the light fittings in British homes will take the EU bulbs so millions of light fittings will have to be replaced. The bulbs cannot be used in ovens, freezers or microwave ovens because they don't work if the temperature is too hot or too cold. And the new bulbs cannot be used in enclosed light fittings because they need more ventilation than the old bulbs. Seventh, the new EU bulbs take ten times as much energy to manufacture as the old ones. Eighth, the new bulbs seem to exacerbate a number of health problems. For example, they can trigger eczema-like skin reactions. Ninth, the EU bulbs need to be broken in for about 100 hours before their brightness level stabilises. Tenth, the bulbs may interfere with the remote control for your television and they may interfere with your radio or cordless telephone. Eleventh, the new bulbs don't last for long if they are turned on and off – to get the best out of them you have to leave them on permanently and learn to sleep with the light on. Twelfth, the EU-approved light bulbs use toxic materials such as mercury vapour. Apart from the fact that the bulbs could be dangerous if they are broken (the British Government has warned that if one of the EU bulbs is smashed the room should be vacated for at least 15 minutes and great care must be taken in clearing up the debris) there is a problem with disposing of dead bulbs. The EU has banned products containing mercury vapour from landfill sites and so used EU bulbs will have to be collected and disposed of separately.

To sum up, the bulbs the EU is forcing us to use are much more dangerous, far more expensive and probably less efficient than the old ones. Should we congratulate the light-bulb industry lobbyists for succeeding in persuading the EU to force over 500 million people to stop using a safe, efficient, cheap product and replace it with what seems to us to be a dangerous, inefficient and expensive one?

As an ironic footnote to this, the EU wants to ban barometers because they contain a small amount of mercury. Barometers have been around for at least 350 years and there is no record of anyone ever having been injured by the mercury inside one. The EU wants all barometers to be broken up and destroyed. The eurocrats do not seem to realise that by doing this they will release all the mercury (now safely contained) into the environment. Despite this attack on barometers, the eurocrats do not seem to mind forcing us to use light-bulbs which contain mercury vapour. Nor do they seem to worry overmuch about the fact that hundreds of millions of individuals in the EU have been vaccinated with vaccines containing mercury. Nor do they seem to worry about the fact that the commonest type of dental filling contains mercury.

8.
The EU Does Not Believe in Democracy
The EU, an organisation which is built on fraud and deceit and which can reasonably claim to be one of the most undemocratic organisations ever invented, has the power to impose direct rule from Brussels on any member country which appears to be in need of better leadership. This is not a theoretical power. The EU has already exercised this power in Greece and Italy. In both countries democratically elected governments were summarily dismissed as surplus to requirements by eurocrats. EU-approved ex-Goldman Sachs administrators were put in charge. In Greece the Prime Minister was thrown out of office when he politely suggested that asking the voters what they thought about it all might be the decent thing to do.

The dislike of democracy seems to affect all those involved in EU issues. When the British House of Lords discussed whether or not the electorate should be allowed a referendum to decide whether or not Britain should remain in the EU, many members of the House of Lords opposed a referendum, claiming that the British public could not be trusted to make the right decision. Lord Mandelson, a former EU commissioner (who is due to receive a generous EU pension) opposed a referendum, claiming that the electorate would be swayed by irrelevant issues. Lord Kinnock, another former EU commissioner with good reason to protect the EU, said that a referendum would be a lame gesture.

Some committed Europhiles readily, almost boastfully, admit that, at times, they have deliberately disguised quite profound changes as mere technical adjustments to avoid annoying EU citizens. According to Jean-Claude Juncker, the Prime Minister of Luxembourg and the EU's longest serving head of government: `We decide on something, leave it lying around and wait and see what happens. If no one kicks up a fuss, because most people don't know what has been decided, we continue step by step until there is no turning back.' It will come as little surprise to impartial observers that the EU plans to ban political parties of which it disapproves.

9.
The EU is Forcing Britain to Become Europe's Dustbin
Waste material which Germany doesn't want to store (because Germans are worried about environmental damage if the waste leaks) is being stored off the British coast. Although other countries won't store the stuff because of safety fears, the EU has ruled that Britain must store the waste instead.

10.
EU Laws, and the European Court of Justice, Now Take Precedence Over Britain's Own Laws (Including the Magna Carta).
Britain now has a Supreme Court (which is often described as `centuries old', as though it were part of English tradition). In reality the Supreme Court was established in October 2009 and is just another piece of EU inspired legislative machinery. The building in which the court is housed may be old but the court itself is hardly old enough to start school. The Supreme Court (a result of the European Convention of Human Rights) has taken over the work of the Law Lords, the Lord Chancellor and part of the Privy Council.

11. British Citizens Can Be Extradited Without the Police Producing Any Evidence of Wrong Doing.
EU laws give every country in the EU the right to arrest any citizen of any other country, except individuals employed by the EU, on suspicion of having broken a law in that country or of having offended that country in any way. (It is now illegal for any EU citizen to criticise the activities of another EU country.) An EU country wanting to arrest a citizen of another EU country does not have to provide any evidence of wrong doing. The crime of which the individual is accused does not have to be a crime in the individual's own country. No court hearings or appeals are required before the extradition process takes place and the offended country does not have to provide evidence of any kind in support of its demand. The arrested citizen can (and will) be taken to the offended country and put in jail to await trial. Within the EU these days there is no presumption of innocence, no habeas corpus and no right to a trial by jury. Recent Prime Ministers who signed up to EU treaties knew all this, even though the European arrest warrant (which enables the police to arrest citizens without anything as inconvenient as `evidence') is directly contrary to the Magna Carta which states: `No free man shall be taken or imprisoned or dispossessed, or outlawed or exiled, or in any way destroyed, nor will we go upon him, nor will we send against him except by lawful judgement of his peers or by the law of the land.'

It is surprising and sad that successive British Governments have allowed the EU to toss aside the Magna Carta because that document provided the foundation for parliamentary democracy around the world. It was also probably not within their legal remit to do this. According to English law the common law rights of citizens cannot be given away by the British parliament and they certainly cannot be revoked by the EU. But, our politicians have ignored history and ridden roughshod over our long-established rights.

The EU is now imposing French legal traditions on Britain and the European Court of Justice (ECJ) which follows the concept of corpus juris, has supplanted our traditional legal system. The ECJ in Strasbourg is a higher court than anything in Britain. It exists, in part at least, to ensure the integration of separate EU countries into the new EU state and it can and does make new laws to govern EU citizens. The EU's legal system will mean the end of all our traditional legal rights. According to our traditions, we are entitled to do those things which are not forbidden, but according to the EU, we are entitled to do those things which are allowed – everything else is forbidden.

In the rapidly developing EU there will be no juries, the authorities will be able to lock us up without trial and if we are eventually brought to court and are found not guilty then the state will be able to keep re-trying us until the `right' verdict is obtained. Thatcher, Major, Blair and Brown should perhaps have been reminded of these words from Winston Churchill: `The power of the executive to cast a man into prison without formulating any charge known to the law, and particularly to deny him the judgement of his peers, is in the highest degree odious and the foundation of all totalitarian government whether Nazi or communist.'

12.
EU Citizens Are Not Entitled To Privacy
Citizens of the EU are not entitled to any privacy. It is, for example, now legal for the police within the EU to have access to medical records in order to protect the organisation and to continue the war on terrorism. Neither patients nor doctors have any right to withhold medical information. It has never been explained why the physical and mental health of individual, law abiding, innocent citizens should be the concern of the police.

The EU has set up a database of individuals who might one day be suspected of breaking EU laws, or who might be suspected of contemplating breaking EU laws. Europol (the EU's own police force) keeps 56 different types of information (including racial origins, religion and political affiliations) on every suspect. Those placed on the list do not need to have committed any crime. And, of course, the EU's extradition programme entitles the police anywhere within the European Union to arrest any citizen without providing any evidence to a court. Nazi inspired and German run, the EU has given us a police force which matches the Gestapo in authority. And unless and until the voters speak out there seems little doubt that things will only get worse.
Even the EU Parliament appears to be alarmed at the extent of the powers given to Europol. In a report entitled `Police and Justice in the EU', the Parliament described Europol as: `the emergence of an embryonic federal system of repression, the creation of a federal police (Europol), a federal prosecutor (Eurojust) and a concept of federal crimes or Eurocrimes. ' The Parliament seemed to

find it most worrying that all the agents of these departments had been given total immunity from prosecution. (Article 5, paragraph 2 of the EU Council Act states: `The officers of the new EU police force, Eurpol, are immune from criminal prosecution should they break the law while carrying out their activities.') Officers in Europol have even greater powers than officers of the Russian KGB. All members of Europol have diplomatic immunity; they can walk into your home, arrest you, beat you up and steal your property and there is not a damned thing you can do about it. Appropriately, one of the Europol buildings was allegedly previously occupied by the Gestapo.

13.
The EU Wastes Vast Quantities of Taxpayers' Money
Fraud is endemic within the EU. Back in 1999 the entire EU Commission was forced to resign because of massive corruption, fraud, theft and incompetence within the EU. (The disgraced commissioners refused to quit for six months and when they did go they kept their pensions.) The EU's own Court of Auditors claimed that £1.1 billion had been misspent and when they tried to investigate, the commissioners explained that documents relating to the relevant year had been destroyed. `Opportunities for fraud are open and they are taken advantage of,' said Marta Andreasen, the EU's former Chief Accountant. She was sacked after complaining of fraud within the EU's accounting systems.

Estimates vary but it seems that fraud costs the EU (which means European taxpayers) a large part of its annual budget (which is in excess of £100 billion a year and set to rise rapidly). VAT fraud within the EU costs European taxpayers another £100 billion a year. Every year billions of euros simply disappear from the EU's accounts. In 2013 alone the European Union wasted £6 billion on fraudulent, illegal or ineligible spending projects. For the 19th year in a row the official auditors refused to approve the EU's accounts or to guarantee their accuracy. Auditors routinely complain that the EU's budget is full of errors and that the failure to follow the correct procedures means that the accounts mess is impossible to untangle. Fraud, corruption and theft are endemic and it does not seem entirely unlikely that money from the EU finds its way into the pockets and campaign funds of politicians who are enthusiastic supporters of the EU project. Money that the EU has given as `grants' to member countries often disappears. Funds that were paid for bridge building and job creation are quite possibly spent on fast cars, expensive wine and luxury holidays. It does not seem at all unfair to conclude that a third of EU employees are corrupt, a third are incompetent and a third are both corrupt and incompetent. If the EU were a company, its directors would by now be serving long prison terms. However, no one employed by the EU is ever prosecuted for theft or dismissed for incompetence because everyone working for the EU has lifetime immunity. EU staff members are untouchable and cannot be investigated, charged or arrested whatever they have done. This immunity continues after their employment has ceased. Buildings occupied by EU officials are also immune – they are `out of bounds' and cannot be searched by the police. The lifetime immunity enjoyed by EU employees means that they cannot be prosecuted whatever they have done – even if they have clearly broken the law.

14.
The Common Agricultural Policy (CAP) Is Dangerously Expensive and Wasteful
The Common Agricultural Policy was designed to provide generous subsidies for French farmers. It is estimated that the CAP costs families throughout Europe over £2,000 a year each. Many people find

it difficult to understand why Britain's first application to join the Common Market was vetoed by General de Gaulle in 1967 when he claimed that Britain was an island and not suited to be a member of a European `superstate'. The French President had, of course, been saved by the British during the Second World War. However, de Gaulle was merely being crafty because he wanted to delay Britain's entry until the Common Agricultural Policy had been set up. Once the CAP was alive and well de Gaulle changed his mind, decided that we were suitable members of a European superstate and encouraged Britain to reapply. He didn't mention it, of course, but he wanted Britain in the Common Market so that we could help pay the massive costs of the CAP and help him pay for inefficient French farming. It is through the CAP that the EU buys up all the excess milk, butter, cereals and so on grown within the EU. The excesses are gathered together as milk lakes and butter mountains and then dumped in other parts of the world. It is this dumping of cheap food which wrecks the farming economies of developing African countries and there is no doubt that the CAP is one of the main causes of poverty and starvation in Africa.

And so, to sum up, the EU's Common Agricultural Policy has dramatically increased the price of food, made life much more difficult for British farmers and resulted in impoverishment and starvation in the Third World.

15.
The EU Wants a 55 Mph Limit on All Roads

The EU is forcing the UK to install even more speed cameras. Another new law will make it a criminal offence for citizens to fail to prevent guests from driving home if they have had too much to drink. The offence (`non prevention of a crime or misdemeanour which causes bodily harm') carries a maximum sentence of five years in prison and a 75,000 euro fine. And the EU Energy Commissioner has called for a 55 mph speed limit throughout Europe. The EU is apparently doing this because eurocrats believe that the reduced speed limit will cut fuel consumption. Sadly, many modern cars are more efficient at 70 mph than they are at 55 mph. A new 55 mph limit would waste time, damage the economy and cause boredom and accidents. It would also result in more fuel being used (and, therefore, in more pollution). But whatever the people want and, whatever the facts may show, the EU always gets what it wants.

16.
The EU Insists That Britain Provide 7,500 Campsites for Travellers

The EU has ruled that local authorities must provide campsites for travellers or gypsies. Councils throughout Britain have been using satellite spy cameras to find private land where they can build gypsy sites. Once suitable land has been found, councils (which have to find 7,500 sites in Britain) use compulsory purchase orders to take the land they have chosen. Even land which has been denied planning permission is being taken to create gypsy campsites. People who object to plans for new sites are invariably dismissed as racist and visited by the police.

17.
The EU Has Abolished Britain's 700-Year-Old Hallmarking System

The EU abolished the traditional gold and silver hallmarking system which had guaranteed the quality of British jewellery for around 700 years and which had made it possible for buyers to identify the age and maker of gold and silver artefacts. Jewellers must now certify the quality of silver and gold with a European standard hallmark.

18.

The EU Wants to Spy On Your Phone Calls and Emails

The EU wants to force all service providers to store customers Internet and telephone data for up to three years. The information stored will include what was said, where you when you said it, lists of all the websites you have visited, details of all your text messages and emails and details of everyone with whom you have communicated.

19.

The EU Wants to Control the Music You Can Listen to

New EU legislation will force musicians to limit the number of pieces of loud music they perform on a single occasion. Orchestras and choirs will have the opportunity to choose to wear earplugs. This new law is part of the Control of Noise at Work Regulations. Concerts will have to be balanced with quieter pieces of music sandwiched between louder works. One eurocrat has said that if orchestras lower the volume during rehearsals they may be able to play at full volume during performances.

20.

The EU Is Changing Our Educational System

New, politically-correct educational systems have been introduced throughout the EU and old-fashioned methods of teaching have been abandoned. Can it possibly be a coincidence that as these new systems have been introduced the quality of education has fallen dramatically throughout the EU countries?

21.

The EU Is Introducing New Tax Laws

The EU has decided that customs officers and tax officials can demand that a tax payer prove himself innocent. The principle of 'innocent until proven guilty' has disappeared. If the authorities say that you are guilty of something then you are guilty unless and until you can prove you are innocent.

The EU intends to control all taxes throughout the European Union. According to the EU: 'unequal tax treatment of equivalent EU taxpayers would probably be considered as discriminatory and against the ideals of EU construction.' EU finance ministers have already set up a working group to work out how best to achieve direct tax harmonisation among EU member countries. There is little doubt that this will lead to the replacement of individual country tax systems with a single EU tax system. Meanwhile, the EU has for several years been planning to augment its own income with its own formidable schedule of taxes. A document released by the European Commission and entitled Tax Based EU Own Resources: An Assessment showed that the EU is looking at nine new EU taxes.

1. An EU personal income tax, probably in the form of a levy on top of national income tax.
2. An EU company tax.
3. An EU tax on road travel.
4. An extension of VAT, with an almost certain end to the zero rating of food, children's clothing, books and public transport.
5. A special EU tax on financial transactions.
6. An EU tax on energy use.
7. An EU tax on air travel.
8. An EU tax on communications.

9. Special EU taxes on alcohol and tobacco.

22.

The EU Is Making DIY Illegal

Under EU regulations it is now illegal for citizens to repair their own plumbing, electrics or motorcar. Trade and industry lobbyists are, of course, suspected of having influenced the EU into making this new law.

23.

The EU Has an Expensive New Law Affecting Boat Buyers

If you live in the EU and buy a boat which is over six feet long and which was built after the EU Recreational Craft Directive of 1999 you must pay the EU £4,000 to measure the boat. If you fail to do this you can be sent to prison for six months.

24.

The EU Will Get Rid of Pints in pubs

The EU has decided that British pubs must throw out all pint glasses which are marked with the crown symbol and replace them with glasses which are marked with the EU's official CE mark. The CE mark stands for Conformite Europeenne and indicates that the manufacturer has satisfied EU requirements for the product concerned. The EU publishes a vast quantity of information about what the CE mark should look like and where it should be placed on each item. Manufacturers who fail to adhere to the EU legislation on product marking must remove their products from the market. They may also be fined and sent to prison though the EU warns that in some circumstances penalties may be greater than `a fine or imprisonment'. They give no hints as to what this might be.

25.

Holiday Home Owners Are Reported As Terrorists or Money Launderers

The EU has told European banks that they must pass details of all international money transfers to the American justice authorities. Britons who have holiday homes in Spain or France and who send money to banks in those countries will be reported to the FBI and the CIA as potential terrorists or money launderers.

26.

EU Rules on Metrication Cause Massive Confusion

There is much confusion among the authorities about when imperial measurements may or may not be used. It is now considered by some to be a criminal offence to use imperial measurements or even to refer to imperial measurements. This is presumably why road signs are being erected without any mileage distances recorded on them. And it is presumably the reason why petrol is sold in litres. (Oddly, however, motor car speed limits are measured in miles.) The British Government, and local councils, have harassed many traders accused of selling vegetables by the pound although the EU has never prohibited the use of weighing instruments manufactured before the year 2000 and capable only of measuring in imperial weights. The whole issue is further confused by the fact that the USA uses imperial measurements and companies wishing to do business with America must sell products which are measured in imperial units.

27.

The EU Has Approved Genetically Modified Food Though There Is No Evidence That It Is Safe

The EU has accepted genetically modified food. The British Government has, of course, rushed to obey the EU and to allow GM foods to be sold in Britain. Other EU countries, such as Austria, Hungary and France, have ignored the EU instruction and banned all genetically modified foods.

28.

The EU Wants Us All To Carry ID Cards

The EU is demanding that we all carry ID cards which carry biometric identification and data. Meanwhile, driving licences and passports will contain a good deal of information which was previously regarded as confidential. Future cards, licences and passports will, if the EU has its way, contain medical records and personal financial information. Your tax inspector will know what illnesses you have had and the receptionist at your doctor's surgery will know how much tax you pay. We will have to carry our ID cards at all times.

29.

The EU Is Changing Our Passports (Again)

British passports have traditionally carried the following words: `Her Britannic Majesty's Secretary of State requests and requires in the Name of Her Majesty all those whom it may concern to allow the bearer to pass freely without let or hindrance, and to afford the bearer such assistance and protection as may be necessary.'

The EU has already replaced our Old Blue passports with rather tawdry little burgundy coloured booklets and naturally, the EU plans to replace this rather old-fashioned nonsense with its own gibberish. The replacement text, as included in the Treaty of Lisbon which was signed by Gordon Brown in 2007 is: `Every citizen of the Union shall, in the territory of a third country in which the members of state of which he is a national is not represented, be entitled to protection by the diplomatic or consular authorities of any member state, on the same conditions as the nationals of that state.'

What this means is that Bulgarians and Romanians will be entitled to be represented by British consular and embassy officials.

30.

The EU's Law on Fridges is Creating a Fridge Mountain

EU regulations forbid the crushing or burying of old fridges. The EU has, however, refused to give any advice on what to do with the unwanted appliances and so millions of unwanted fridges are now rotting in piles on car parks and fields. These old fridges are a major cause of pollution. In England alone the pile of unwanted fridges is growing at a rate of 2,500,000 a year.

31.

EU Has Banned Firemen's Poles to Protect the Disabled

Firemen's poles have been banned by the EU because eurocrats feared that firemen might hurt themselves when sliding down them. It was also decreed that the poles (and, presumably, the holes around them) might prove to be a hazard to blind or otherwise disabled employees. Thanks to the anonymous eurocrat who thought this one up it now takes considerably longer for firemen to leave their fire stations and reach their fire engines.

32.
The EU Has Introduced New EU Laws on Abattoir Inspection
British abattoirs are inspected by British meat inspectors, but the EU has ruled that the British inspectors must be supervised by official EU experts. Many of the EU experts (known as `vets') have received just one week's training.

33.
The EU Only Allows What it Allows
When the EU first began it was decided that everything permitted should be written down and everything not written down should not be allowed.

34.
The EU Even Has a Law On Duck Eggs
The EU directive on duck eggs (which regulates the shape and size of duck eggs) runs to 26,911 words. By comparison the Ten Commandments and Abraham Lincoln's Gettysburg address are around 300 words each.

35.
The EU Has Decided How Many Hours You Can Work
The EU working time directive, which rules that no one should work more than 35 hours a week, applies to everyone. The idea behind it was that if working hours were regulated, no country would have an advantage over another because its people were prepared to work hard. The plan was that a standardised working week would help turn the EU into a single nation. Moreover, the eurocrats who thought this one up (and who presumably had little or no experience at all of real life) argued that a shorter working week would mean less unemployment. (The eurocrats recently announced that the self-employed would be exempt from this law though this may have been because they had, finally, realised how difficult it would be to police the working hours of individuals working for and by themselves.) Unfortunately, the eurocrats did not realise that their law would have fearful consequences. For example, it did not occur to them that their new law would result in many companies going bust and having to fire everyone.

36.
The EU Parliament Is a Farce
The EU Parliament is not much of a democratic institution. MEPs merely press buttons in order to vote and on one occasion a staggering 287 votes were taken in just over an hour. Criticisms are edited out of Parliamentary reports because they are considered embarrassing. Most astonishing of all MEPs who are absent from the chamber during voting are assumed to have voted in favour of every resolution. Their votes are counted in support of all the motions they have missed. Democracy, EU style.

37.
The EU Has Destroyed the NHS

The EU has done enormous damage to the quality of medical care in Britain. It is because of the EU that general practitioners no longer provide 24 hour cover for their patients and it is because of the EU that hundreds of thousands of hospital patients go for several days at a time without seeing a doctor at all. There is no doubt that laws which came from the EU are responsible for thousands of deaths and much misery.

The EU law which has done the most damage has, of course, been the 'working time directive' which has put strict, legal limits on the number of hours doctors and nurses are allowed to work. It is because of this legislation that the modern doctor works the sort of hours traditionally associated with librarian and local council employees. If hospital doctors work more hours than the EU permits then the hospital must pay a huge fine. The result of this legal nonsense is that doctors have to abandon patients in the middle of treating them and at weekends there are often no doctors available at all. The EU has made things even worse by ruling that if doctors are asleep but on call then they are 'working' even if they are not woken up. To make sure that doctors obey the EU legislation, hospitals employ Working Time Directive Project Managers (on salaries in excess of £50,000) whose sole job is to make sure that doctors clock off on time and don't spend a moment more than the EU allows on looking after patients. The NHS spends an estimated £250,000,000 a year policing the Working Time Directive to satisfy the demands of EU eurocrats. The EU law limiting the number of hours doctors work has had many consequences. For instance, whereas, just a few years ago, doctors who became consultants usually had 30,000 hours of experience and training, today's young doctors can become consultants after just 6,000 hours of experience and training. So, today's consultants have one fifth the experience of their predecessors. It is largely because of the EU's law that inadequately trained nurses have been given the authority to prescribe drugs, provide anaesthesia and perform operations. And it is, of course, the absurd EU legislation on working hours which is responsible for the fact that GPs (limited now to a standard working week) no longer remain on call at evening, weekends or on bank holidays. (A growing number of patients who need emergency care now obtain their diagnoses and their prescriptions from doctors working via the internet.)

Incidentally, Foundation Hospitals were created within the NHS because the EU told the British Government that if Britain joins the euro the NHS must be broken up into a series of regionally controlled hospitals and clinics. The creation of Foundation Hospitals was considered a useful preliminary move.

38.

EU Laws on Airports Will Close Many Small Airports

The EU has made it illegal for small airports to encourage small airlines. This has been done to help protect large airlines which do not use small airports. As a result of this legislation it seems likely that many small regional airports will close.

39.

The EU is Introducing New Driving Licence Laws

The EU is planning to abolish British driving licences. Britons who want to drive will have to take a test (and pay a fee) every ten years. Anyone with a medical problem will have to take a medical test (and pay a fee) to prove that they are fit to drive. The new look driving licence (including the EU ring of stars logo) was designed according to rules provided by the EU.

40.

The EU Has Changed Vehicle Log Books

The Driver and Vehicle Licensing Agency in Swansea has issued new Vehicle Registration Certificates which have been developed (at huge cost) to `comply with a European Directive which requires member states to introduce a common format for Registration Certificates.

41.

EU Law Results in Old Cars Being Abandoned

Cars which passed their drive by date were, in the past, sold to scrap dealers who would often collect the wreck and pay a few pounds for it. Today, thanks to new EU laws about the ways in which cars can be scrapped, owners must pay to have their vehicles taken away. As a result our countryside is littered with unwanted and often burnt out car wrecks.

42.

The EU Intends to Force Motorists to Drive With Their Headlights on

The EU intends to introduce a new law forcing motorists to keep their headlights on all day long. Motorists who drive without keeping their headlights on will be fined and may accumulate points which will result in the loss of their driving licence. There is, of course, no evidence to show that this will save lives or protect the environment. The EU consulted the 495 million inhabitants of the EU and received responses from 117 individuals who were overwhelmingly opposed to the plan. So the EU will be going ahead with it and there will, presumably, be many happy lobbyists working for the headlamp bulb industry.

43.

EU Furniture Laws Mean Waste

EU laws mean that furniture must be thrown away if it doesn't have an EU-approved fire certificate. As a result vast quantities of perfectly useable furniture is burnt, buried or dumped in a lay-by.

44.

EU's Drinking Laws Cause Drunkenness and Street Crime

Britain's drinking laws have been revised to fit in with drinking laws throughout the EU. As a result street crime and drunkenness are rising dramatically in many areas.

45.

EU's Banking Laws Make Life Difficult for Bank Customers

The absurd rigmarole through which customers must go when trying to open a new bank account, or to move their own money from one account to another, is a direct result of EU legislation designed (so it is said) to control money laundering.

46.

The EU Has Changed School Examinations

Changes to school examinations were made to fit in with school diplomas elsewhere in the EU.

47.

EU Staff Can Create Whatever New Laws They Want to Create

The Treaty of Lisbon, which Gordon Brown signed on Britain's behalf, gives unelected eurocrats working for the EU the authority to create whatever laws they want to create. It is interesting to note that Adolf Hitler had similar powers, having given himself the authority to issue laws as and when he saw fit. Brown and other British politicians claimed that the Treaty of Lisbon was of so little constitutional significance that there was no need to hold a referendum in Britain to discuss its contents. Citizens were repeatedly assured that the Treaty was simply a tidying up exercise.

It was, of course, Hitler who wrote that people `more readily fall victims to the big lie than the small lie, since it would never come into their heads to fabricate colossal untruths, and they would not believe that others could have the impudence to distort the truth so infamously.' In addition to his view about the size of a lie being important Hitler also claimed that if a lie was to be believed it should be repeated as often as possible. He argued that if lies were repeated frequently they would, eventually, be confused with the truth by the greater part of the population.

48.

EU Tobacco Laws Exhibit Rank Hypocrisy

The EU has wisely banned tobacco companies from sponsoring sporting events within the EU. And it is EU legislation which forces office workers who want to smoke to stand on the pavement in the rain.

But for decades the EU has paid out billions of pounds in subsidies to European tobacco farmers – to encourage them to grow cheaper tobacco.

Sadly, much of the tobacco grown by European farmers has always been so rich in tar and nicotine that it has been unsuitable for sale within the EU. And so this tobacco has been sold to Third World and Eastern block countries. It has, of course, been sold at very low prices because its production has been subsidised by European taxpayers.

49.

EU Has Destroyed Britain's Fishing Industry

Just before Britain joined the EU, the existing members suddenly agreed to a new principle: equal access to `community' fishing waters. Since Britain is an island which traditionally relies on fishing this sudden change in the laws should have sent our politicians back to the negotiating table. Changing an important part of a contract at the last moment is a long-established negotiating tactic commonly used by crooks such as Robert Maxwell. But Edward Heath was desperate to sign up and receive his £35,000 pay off and so he said nothing, treating our fishing industry as expendable.

Today, it is widely agreed that the EU's common fisheries policy is a shambles. It has ruined the British fishing industry and created a social, economic and environmental disaster. As a result of the EU's laws, most of the important fishing areas around Britain have been dangerously over-fished. And although EU quota systems mean that cheaper fish must be thrown back into the sea most of these fish are dead by the time they reach the water.

50.

The Cost of the EU Rises Inexorably

The cost of our membership of the EU is impossible to measure in purely financial terms (EU laws on immigration, working hours, rubbish collection and so on affect our lives in every imaginable way) but there is no doubt that the pure financial cost is considerable. The net cost of our membership of the EU rises regularly but the best available estimate is that it costs the UK around £77 billion a year to retain its membership of the European Union. That is the net cost after EU grants to the UK have been taken into consideration. Pro EU campaigners will often claim that the EU provides financial benefits to the UK in the form of trade with EU members. Such claims are, of course, sheer nonsense. It is absurd to imagine that, if the UK left the EU, the remaining EU members would be unwilling to trade with us. (We spend more buying goods and services from other EU countries than they spend buying goods and services from us.)

51.

The Truth about EU Grants

Some areas of Britain have received grants from the EU – usually for specific projects which can be labelled as having been supported with EU funds. The result is that many people point to these projects when explaining just how useful our membership of the EU has been. What is never pointed out, however, is that for every £1 which the EU hands out the British taxpayer will have already paid £2 to the EU. And every time the EU provides a grant of £1 the British taxpayers must provide another £1 to match the EU's contribution.

52.

EU Rules That Prisoners Should Be Allowed to Vote

The EU has ruled that prisoners must be allowed to vote. In some parts of the country, where prison populations are exceptionally high, it seems likely that political representatives will be voted into office by prisoners.

53.

The EU Law on Ponies Will Result in Wild Ponies Disappearing

The EU has ruled that every pony in Britain – even the wild ones on Dartmoor and Exmoor – must have an expensive health certificate issued by a vet. The new law is being introduced because ponies are eaten in many EU countries and must, therefore, be regulated, approved and stamped.

54.

EU Laws on Homosexuals and Transsexuals

Although British politicians often take the credit for pushing through legislation allowing homosexuals to marry, and allowing transsexuals to change their birth certificates so that they can marry, the truth is that these new laws were issued by the EU.

55.

The EU is Responsible for Our Disappearing Freedom of Speech

When five Britons visited Brussels and drove around the city in vehicles which carried posters calling for a referendum on the EU constitution they were arrested for `disturbing public order' and `demonstrating without permission'. The European Court of Justice has decreed that the EU commission can restrict dissent and punish individuals who damage the institution's image and reputation or who criticise its leading figures. (So far the EU has seemed fairly reluctant to use this legislative power – presumably because it wouldn't look very good if it did. But the law is there and the EU can, and undoubtedly will, use it.)

56.
EU Laws Provide Privacy for Politicians
The European Community Directive 95/46 exists to protect public figures such as politicians and allows them to prevent newspapers and others printing material about them that they don't want to see in print.

57.
EU Laws Close Shops and Create Long Queues
It is because of EU regulations that many small shops now operate shorter working hours and are closed one or even two days a week. It is because of EU regulations that shops and other businesses (such as doctors' surgeries) close at lunchtime. And it is because of EU regulations that an increasing number of shops now fill their shops with little mazes so that customers waiting to be served can stand in line neatly. (It is for the same reason that many shops are now introducing self-service tills – with the result that the number of employment opportunities in the retail trade will fall dramatically.)

58.
EU Law Forces Pig Owners to Apply for Walking Licenses
Pig owners who want to take their pig for a walk must apply for an EU licence. On orders from Brussels, the British Government introduced the `Pigs (Records, Identification and Movement) Order 2003' which tells pig owners that if they want to take their pig for a walk they must apply for a pig walking licence. Pig owners who wish to walk their pigs must also notify the Ministry before each outing so that an official can visit and inspect the proposed route. This new legislation apparently applies only to pigs.

59.
EU Law Forces Britain to Employ an Army of Translators
The EU has 24 official languages. All EU documents must be translated into all 24 languages. The EU employs an army of translators to make sure that the Swedes know what the Maltese are saying and that the Lithuanians understand the Fins. Britain must also provide an army of translators so that documents can be made available in 24 languages for those immigrants who do not want to learn English.

60.
The EU Does Not Approve of Small Businesses
The EU, like all fascist organisations, does not approve of `small' anything. And so small businesses, small hospitals, small medical centres, small shops and small post offices are all disappearing. This is not an accident or a coincidence. It is a result of EU policy. Large organisations can be controlled far

more efficiently than small ones and can be fitted more comfortably into the statist world of the European Union.

61.

EU Laws on Vegetables

Defenders of the EU often claim that critics have exaggerated the absurd nature of many EU laws. Not true. For example, European Union Directive 2257/94 states that it is a `criminal offence to sell bananas of abnormal curvature' and `European Union Directive 1677/88 refers to the curvature of cucumbers. There are, in addition, directives ruling that peaches picked between July and October must not be less than 5.6 centimetres in diameter, that Class 1 Victoria plums must measure 3.5 centimetres across and that carrots which are less than 1.9 centimetres wide at the thick end are not allowed unless they are sold as a special variety of baby carrot. And tomatoes must be between 53 and 63 millimetres in diameter. There are constantly changing requirements for potatoes. The result of these laws is that vast amounts of perfectly edible food is thrown away and many thousands of hours are wasted measuring vegetables to make sure that EU directives are obeyed. (The word `directive' and `regulation' are used by eurocrats because they seem to sound less frightening than `law' but in practice there is no difference between a `directive', a `regulation' and a `law'.)

62.

EU Laws Make Life Impossible for Employers

During recent years the EU has introduced a vast amount of legislation controlling the way in which employers can run their businesses. A tiny proportion of this legislation may help to protect employees against unscrupulous employers. Most of it, however, puts unbearable burdens on small employers. Legislation which forces employers to allow female members of staff to take a year off work after childbirth (and to have their job kept open for them) may work well enough at the EU's headquarters but prove impossibly difficult for employers running small businesses with a handful of employees. The new laws arrive thick and fast. New fathers are entitled to take time off work. The EU has ruled that staff who fall ill while they are on holiday must be given extra holiday time to make up for the holiday they have lost through illness. Employees with disabled relatives or friends are entitled to take off as much time as they think they need. An employee with a disabled neighbour must be allowed to take the time off work if the neighbour needs taking to the dentist – however inconvenient this may be for the employer. According to the law there are already six million officially designated `carers' in Britain.

It is illegal to make employees redundant if they become blind or deaf (even if this means that they cannot do the work they are paid to do). And if an employee wants to write a book there is a law which says he or she should be allowed to take all the time they need to satisfy their creative urges.

If an employer says he is going to expand, and then changes his mind, he will be breaking the law if he does not hire the people he said he thought he would hire. If an employer wants to change the way his business is run he must ask his employees for their approval. If employees complain that they have not been properly consulted the employer can be fined up to £75,000 for each offence. So, a newsagent who decides to start selling chewing gum but fails to obtain approval from his two employees could face a fine of £150,000. If an employer decides he cannot cope then he must consult his employees and obtain their approval before he closes down his business. If an employer does want to hire someone new then he cannot say that he is looking for a man or a woman or a young person or an old person. One employer found himself in trouble by paying for an advertisement saying that he was looking for a `hard worker'. He was told that this was illegal because it discriminated against people who are not hard workers. Employers must make sure that boring and repetitive work is eliminated and that employees have a say about the way they do their work and the number of breaks they take. It is, perhaps, hardly surprising that three out of five new businesses now fail within the first three years. And it is less surprising that most of the people whose businesses fail blame the same factor: increasing interference and red tape.

It is not, of course, only private businesses which suffer. Local councils must also obey all these laws and it has been reported that, thanks to EU employment policies, public libraries now spend 54% of their budgets on staff and just 9% on buying books. Bureaucracy means that it costs a local library £24 to buy a book with a retail cover price of £10.

The eurocrats who think up all this nonsense work in an environment where money is no object and where employees can disappear for years at a time without anyone noticing. No eurocrat seems to understand that employers also have responsibilities to customers, other employees and, indeed, themselves and their families. And no one working for the EU seems to care that the biggest employers have for years been getting round EU legislation by hiring part-time employees on short-term contracts. It does not seem to occur to anyone that for many people the EU legislation has resulted in less security and fewer rights.

63.

EU Laws on Religion

There is an EU law which makes it an offence to put up Christmas cards which feature nativity scenes. There is an EU law which makes it possible for workers to object to Christmas decorations on the grounds that they create an offensive working environment. Workers whose religion involves abstaining from alcohol now have the right to complain (and to seek compensation) if a fellow worker is seen handing a bottle of wine to a colleague as a gift. Employees must be given time off work for religious holidays, festivals and prayers. The legislation lists 81 specific religious festivals which must be recognised. Employers who do not provide prayer rooms for different religions are breaking the law.

64.

EU Staff Treat Themselves to a Luxury Lifestyle

The EU has around 55,000 employees who enjoy large salaries, hefty expense accounts and huge pensions. Very few of these are British. EU employees are exempt from income tax (or any other form of tax) and enjoy more holidays than schoolteachers. When it became clear that the EU region was heading for terrible financial problems the leaders of individual EU countries wrote to the European Commission requesting that the EU increase its spending by no more than inflation and suggesting that the EU might consider reducing the absurdly high salaries paid to EU officials and increasing their working week. The response to the suggestion and the request was an imperious wave of two fingers.

In September 2011, it was announced that EU staff were refusing to work a 40 hour week. They claimed that working so hard would ruin the attractiveness of their jobs. The 55,000 EU officials refused even to discuss working as many as 40 hours a week. EU officials can earn between £104,000 and £185,000 a year and have three months holiday a year. They are given an extra 24 days off work every year if they put in an extra 45 minutes at the office (although this can be spent chatting or surfing the Web). They also get seven days of public holidays and an additional 11 non-working days when the EU offices are closed at Christmas. A union representative, explaining the long holidays, said that 'the principle of recuperation needs to be consolidated'. Most of these people would be of much more use to society if they were set to work manning tills in supermarkets and our few remaining high street retailers.

Diplomats working in Baroness Ashton's EU foreign service are entitled to 17 weeks holiday a year. They are also entitled to two weeks off for 'professional training'. As if that wasn't enough, diplomats working in the 30 EU delegations in the Far East, Asia and Africa are also entitled to another four or five weeks off work. If they have to travel further than the nearest five star restaurant they are entitled to two days travelling time and paid business class tickets for themselves and their families. Their accommodation is free of charge and their extraordinary high salaries are paid largely tax free.

Finally, as if all this holiday were not enough for them, European Commission officials each took, on average, 14.6 sick days in 2013. That is triple the number of sick days that British private sector workers take and twice the number of sick days that public sector workers take. It doesn't seem to be an exaggeration to say that some EU staff members must be away from their offices more than they are in them.

65.

EU Laws on Health and safety

Most of the absurd health and safety laws which have been introduced in recent years were dreamt up by unelected eurocrats. The cost and inconvenience of satisfying these endless demands cannot be measured. But what can be measured is the incidence of accidents. Despite a plethora of laws designed to stop people tap dancing in high heels on the top of stepladders, or tying their shoe laces while standing on window ledges, the incidence of accidental injury continues to rise remorselessly. It isn't difficult to explain this apparent paradox. Too many rules and regulations stop people using their common sense.

66.

The EU Plans To Abolish Greenwich Mean Time

The EU wants us to get rid of Greenwich Mean Time so that we can match our clocks to those in France and Germany. Our Government will suggest that they are considering whether or not to accede to this demand but they do not, of course, have any choice in the matter. The EU Rules.

67.

The EU Has Made European Travel More Difficult

Those who adore the EU claim that the EU has made it much easier for travellers to move around Europe. This is clearly nonsense. It is now far more difficult for Britons to travel to mainland Europe than it was 20, 30, 40 or 50 years ago. The queues at airports and railway stations are far, far longer than ever before and the customs staff who examine passports and baggage, and who have been endowed with extraordinary powers, are more aggressive than their predecessors. EU laws, ostensibly designed to halt money laundering and terrorism, simply frustrate and delay honest citizens trying to conduct business or go on holiday.

68.

The EU's Rubbish Laws Have Turned Us Into Unpaid Labourers

For most people few things have had as great an impact on their lives as the EU's laws about the collecting of rubbish. We used to put our rubbish in bins which were emptied by dustmen. The dust lorries took our rubbish to tips and it was then either used to fill in old mines or quarries or used to reclaim land from the sea. But the EU has banned this apparently sensible use of waste and now insists that we recycle all our rubbish. In principle this seems a good idea, though in practice what happens is that millions of tons of the rubbish carefully collected for recycling is exported to China where it is put into mines or used to reclaim land from the sea.

Our Government and local councils pay great attention to the EU laws on rubbish recycling because the EU has given itself the authority to fine us hundreds of millions of pounds if we breach their laws on how much rubbish we send to landfill sites.

In their attempts to deal with the EU legislation councils have produced a mass of often absurd and invariably counter-productive legislation of their own. Householders are told that they must clean and sort their rubbish and place it in a variety of plastic bags or containers. In some parts of the country householders, who are frequently bombarded with printed instructions, must sort their rubbish into nine different bags.

The problems caused by this new legislation are many but it is difficult to deny that the whole crazy recycling fad has done far more harm than good. Cutting rubbish collections to once a fortnight means that rubbish lies around in the streets for long periods, attracting rats and spreading disease. Telling householders to double wrap their waste means that even more plastic is wasted. Our former method of dealing with old car batteries resulted in 97% of batteries being recycled. The new, EU method, means that the number of batteries recycled has fallen under 80%. No one has bothered to explain to consumers just how they are supposed to reduce the amount of rubbish they produce when manufacturers double or triple wrap almost everything they make. Billions of gallons of water are wasted on washing out tin cans, jam jars and yoghurt cartons for no one in authority seems to realise that water, our most valuable commodity, is in short supply.

The disaster began in 1987 when a European Treaty allowed the EU to control how we dispose of our waste. Denmark and Holland were running out of space in which to bury their rubbish and, in order to cater for their very specific needs, the European Commission introduced new laws covering the whole of the EU. As usual with the EU the policy they produced, the Landfill Directive of 1999, was a mixture of misunderstanding, ignorance and compromise and it has created chaos, confusion and anger.

The eurocrats decided that since Holland and Denmark didn't have any space in which to bury their rubbish we should all phase out burying our rubbish in holes in the ground (regardless of whether or not we had enough empty holes) and instead start incinerating rubbish or recycling it. Britain suffered more than most countries in the EU because whereas other countries have, in the past, favoured incineration we have always favoured using rubbish for landfill. We had always done more sensible recycling than any other European country.

Today, the whole business of forcing homeowners to spend time sorting through their rubbish like slum dwellers scavenging on a landfill site is cruel and absurd. Millions of people spend several hours a week separating bottles from tins and cardboard from paper. The cost of all this wasted time to the economy must be measured in billions. The cost of the wasted water must be added to that. The fact is, however, that everyone in the waste industry knows that it is far cheaper and far more efficient to sort waste by machine. It is even possible to buy a machine which can separate different types and colours of plastic. Over 288 million tons of waste are collected in the UK each year but only about 11% of that is household waste. The remaining 89% of the waste is collected from businesses and it is collected unsorted. Machines do the sorting and they do it at least twice as well as people can manage.

It is the EU directive which forces home owners to waste their time doing something that can be done more speedily and more efficiently by machine. The relevant EU law says that member states should ensure 'that waste is separately collected if technically, environmentally and economically practicable'. And so that is what the Government and the councils force us all to do. From the beginning of January 2015 things will get even worse because then the number of categories will increase yet again. It's difficult to avoid the suspicion that the EU forces us to waste our time needlessly sorting our rubbish so that we don't have time to contemplate the truth about the reasons behind the awful world the EU is creating for us.

69.

The EU's Building Regulations Have Pushed up House Prices and Restricted House Building

During the last decade the EU has introduced a mass of new restrictions and building regulations which have added enormously to the cost of building new houses. Between the years 1997 and 2004 the cost of building a new house rose by over 60%, with much of this increase coming directly from the new regulations and restrictions introduced by the EU. It is hardly surprising that we are building far too few new homes for our country's expanding needs. The EU has given us, through its immigration policies, a dramatically rising population and, through its house building regulations, a dramatically reduced number of houses in which to home them. The EU is also responsible for imposing building standards which requires the Government to knock down well-built Victorian houses. The building industry welcomes these new laws (and probably lobbies for them) for the same reason that the motor industry welcomes stricter regulations governing motor vehicles.

70.

The EU is Destroying Britain's Farming Industry

The EU forbids British farmers to produce enough milk for the country's needs. However, farmers in France, Germany and Ireland are all allowed to produce more milk than their citizens require. The result is that British farms are suffering twice. They are limited in the amount of milk they can produce and the surplus brought in from abroad means that the price paid to British farmers inevitably falls.

The EU has also encouraged the development of huge farming conglomerates. The EU prefers large farms, or Soviet style collectives, because these are better able to produce acceptably shaped crops. Ten years ago there were 5,000 farms producing potatoes. Today there are just 250 potato growers. Thanks to the EU a thousand farmers and farm workers leave the land every week and join the growing millions on benefits.

What the eurocrats don't seem to realise is that smaller farmers actually produce more food per acre than large ones. Farmers who work on small areas learn to intercrop plants and to rotate their crops more efficiently.

The great sadness, of course, is that as the planet's oil disappears the big farms (which rely heavily on oil based fertilisers and oil run machinery) will run into serious trouble. And there will be very few men and women capable of running small farms.

71.

The EU Wrecks Pensions for Non EU Employees

People who live within the EU but who neither work for the EU or a Government department are going to be much poorer in their old age as a result of new legislation introduced by the EU. In 2007 the EU introduced a law which meant that pension funds had to change the way they invested their money. The direct result of that legislation is that pension funds are now much poorer than they used to be. And so the pensions that will be available in the future will be much smaller. EU employees, however, will be unaffected by this legislation.

72.

The EU is Awash with Quangos

The European Commissioners control a vast number of quangos which provide well-paid jobs and pensions for a rapidly growing bureaucracy. Supporters of the EU are often rewarded with a position on a quango. Well-known quangos include: `The EU Institute for Gender Equality', `The European Monitoring Centre on Racism and Xenophobia' and `The Community Plant Variety Office'. There is a `European Food Safety Authority' and a `European Railways Agency'. In addition, there are also over 3,000 secret working groups feeding opinions and advice to the Commissioners. All these groups have the authority to tell British civil servants what to do, and so British taxpayers are now paying British civil servants to do what EU civil servants tell them to do.

73.

The EU is Changing the Laws on Wills

The EU wants Britons to make wills which are EU friendly and so eurocrats have prepared common principles for will makers. The eurocrats have decided that a `European Certificate of Inheritance' must be introduced. The EU's plans will undoubtedly mean that British inheritance laws will have to be abandoned. The new EU law about inheritance will mean that French laws will be introduced and that Britons will be forced to spread their estate among close relatives. (In France this has resulted in large farm estates being split into tiny and often impractical holdings.)

Appendix One: The Lisbon Treaty

The latest version of the EU constitution (The Lisbon Treaty) was signed by Gordon Brown in December 2007.

Both Brown and his predecessor Tony Blair claimed that the there was no need for a referendum before signing the Treaty since it made very little difference to anything. Jack Straw, the British Foreign Minister, said that the Lisbon Treaty would bolster Britain's sovereign rights. The Labour Government claimed that the new constitution was merely a tidying up exercise.

However, now that the Lisbon Treaty has been signed, Britain no longer has control over its own finances, foreign policy, taxation policies, defence, education social security, criminal justice, immigration, transport, asylum seekers, heath care, transport, communications, business policies, energy policies or, indeed, anything else that matters. The new constitution gives the EU unlimited powers. Jean-Luc Dehaene, Vice President of the Convention which drafted the constitution said: `The EU constitution represents `a great step forward for the EU to become a true political union'. Josep Borrell, the President of the European Parliament announced proudly that `This constitution marks a shift from a primarily economic Europe to a political Europe.' And it is difficult to argue with them. After all the new constitution states: `The EU law shall have primacy over the law of member States.' And `Member States shall actively and unreservedly support the European Union's foreign and security policy.'

After Brown had betrayed Britain and signed the treaty a report by the House of Commons foreign affairs select committee concluded that the Treaty had ceded vital powers to Brussels and that ministers had misled the public by saying that it did not. The committee accused the Government of downplaying the importance of the provisions in the treaty.

But it was too late.

The Lisbon Treaty which Brown signed proposed a more powerful EU army, a huge rise in the EU budget, Europe wide taxes, a massive increase in workers' rights (including a guarantee of jobs for life), a common education curriculum throughout the EU (to include pro-EU propaganda), a more powerful EU army, full control over immigration policies and recognition that the new constitution be regarded as the first step towards political unity.

It was later revealed, in a confidential EU paper, that although Gordon Brown had signed the Lisbon Treaty he hadn't really known what it meant because the EU had not decided precisely what powers it would take. `Much of the Lisbon Treaty is about giving the EU power to create new institutions and arrangements and to decide on how they will actually work in practice at a later date,' said a European think tank.

It wasn't the first time signatories to an EU Treaty had signed a blank cheque. When the first Treaty of Rome was signed it consisted of a very impressive collection of blank pages. There was a frontispiece and a page for signatures. The rest was blank paper, to be filled in later.

Appendix Two: Important dates in the history of the European Union.

Although they are (understandably) usually omitted from official histories of the European Union it is clear that Benito Mussolini and Adolf Hitler were the real founders of the EU.

1933: Benito Mussolini, the Italian leader, talks of the need for political unity among the countries of Europe.

1936: Adolf Hitler, the German leader, calls for Europe to adopt one legal system. He devises   the phrase a `United States of Europe' to explain his plan.

1940: Reichsmarschall Herman Goering (leading member of the Nazi party and later to become Hitler's deputy) devises the name `European Economic Community' for the planned pan-European organisation.

1940: Walther Funk, banker and economics adviser to Hitler, prepares a memo entitled `Economic Reorganisation of Europe' and has the idea of introducing a standard currency to be used in European countries.

1942: The Nazi party publishes a document entitled `Basic Elements of a Plan for the New Europe' and proposes `harmonisation of labour conditions and social welfare' among European countries.

1942: Reinhard Heydrich, high ranking Nazi official and one of the main architects of the Holocaust, publishes `The Reich Plan for the Domination of Europe' (which bears a remarkable similarity to the later Treaty of Rome).

1943: Thirteen countries (including France and Italy) are invited to join a new European Federation under German military control.

1944: A Nazi conference is held in Berlin entitled: `How Will Germany Dominate the Peace When it Loses the War?' Money is sent to America for safe keeping. Another meeting is held in Strasbourg (now the headquarters of the European Union).

1952: The European Coal and Steel Community is created as a result of the Paris Treaty.

1957: The Rome Treaty (also known as The Treaty of Rome) is signed. The original signatories are Belgium, France, Italy, Luxembourg, Netherlands and Germany. The result is the European Economic Community or EEC (widely known as the Common Market).

1958: The European Commission is created as an unelected, unaccountable executive cabinet to `run' the EEC. Commissioners have the exclusive right to put forward new legislation and to decide how the EU should operate. The aim of the Commissioners is to boost the power of the EU and the speed the rate at which the federal state is developed. The unelected commissioners are nominated by their governments. Britain's recent appointees include such political luminaries as Neil Kinnock and Peter Mandelson – both of whom seemed to fit well into the EU system. (NB The European Commission should not be confused with the European Council which is a body made up of the heads of the EU's member countries.)

1961: President John F Kennedy of the USA tells UK Prime Minister Harold Macmillan that the USA will support Britain's application to join the EEC if the goal is political integration.

1967: The Merger Treaty is signed. This creates a single set of institutions to run the European Community.

1973: Prime Minister Edward Heath takes Britain into the Common Market without asking the approval of the British People. Heath pushes the European Communities Bill through the House of Commons as an ordinary vote. (There are many who believe that Britain's membership of the EU breached constitutional convention and was, consequently, illegal.) Just before the 1970 election which had made him Prime Minister, Edward Heath had declared that it would be wrong if any Government contemplating membership of the European Community were to take this step without 'the full-hearted consent of Parliament and the people'. The prospect of a £35,000 reward for pushing Britain into the EU without the consent of the people may have helped Heath change his mind.

1975: The British people are invited to approve membership of the Common Market. Harold Wilson tries to correct Heath's constitutional error by organising a retrospective referendum. The campaign for a 'yes' vote is supported by most of the press and a huge grant from the Common Market.

1986: The Single European Act is signed by Margaret Thatcher.

1992: The Maastricht Treaty is signed by John Major.

1997: The Amsterdam Treaty is signed by Tony Blair, turning the EEC into the European Union.

1999: The Eurozone (for countries replacing their traditional currency with the euro) is introduced in 1999 and comes into full force in 2002.

2001: The Nice Treaty is signed by Tony Blair.

2007: The Lisbon Treaty is signed by Gordon Brown finally creating a single legal entity and creating a permanent President of the European Council. The Lisbon Treaty provides a new, final constitution for the EU and opens the door for a political union of the member States. Hitler's dream of a United States of Europe has now become a reality – although in many ways the organisation which has been created bears a greater resemblance to the former United States of Soviet Republics (USSR).

Appendix Three: How We Would Benefit If We Left the EU

Despite all the treaties which have been signed it would be easy for Britain to leave the European Union. Parliament simply has to repeal the Acts of Parliament which have been signed (probably illegally) and to tell the EU that they can have their flag back. The EU is hardly likely to complain too much – they have always regarded our island as an addendum to Europe – and it would not look good if they started a war to force us to retain our membership. There is no doubt that all Britons would be better off (in every conceivable way) outside the EU. Only politicians (looking forward to large pay outs from the EU) and executives (running large, international businesses and looking forward to persuading the EU to create new, business-friendly legislation) benefit from the EU. Here are just a few of the ways in which just about everyone would benefit if we left the EU.

1. We would no longer have to pay several billion pounds a year to the EU as the direct price of our subscription. (If Scotland wants to leave the UK there would be nothing to stop it applying for membership of the EU in its own right.) Our membership of the EU has already cost us hundreds of billions of pounds. We have received nothing in return for this money – except a good many new laws we don't like and didn't want. The total cost of our membership of the EU (including the cost of the higher prices produced by EU laws relating to food and energy) is many billions of pounds a year.

2. We would have control over our own immigration policies. Since we joined the EU immigration has shot up from a manageable 30,000 a year to an unmanageable two to three million a year.

3. We would regain our freedom, our right to celebrate our history, our culture and our own flag. We would regain our sovereignty.

4. We would lose well over 150,000 laws foisted on us by unelected EU eurocrats.

5. We would be able to deal with our rubbish in a sane and sensible way.

6. We would regain control of our energy policies and household energy bills would drop dramatically.

7. Household food bills would be noticeably lower.

8. Unemployment levels in Britain would fall. Our manufacturing trade deficit with the EU is now huge. The highly promoted `single market' has moved British jobs to Eastern Europe and led to rising unemployment in Britain. Europhiles claim that leaving the EU would lead to a rise in unemployment but this is not true. EU regulations affect 100% of our economy but only 10% of our goods are exported to the EU. We should remember that English is the world's leading language and the language of the internet. Our language advantage means that we can trade easily with any other country in the world.

9. We would regain power over our agricultural policies.

10. Europhiles claim that if we left the EU then other countries would be less keen to invest in Britain. This is nonsense. If we were outside the EU, and free of the endless bureaucracy which is stifling business, Britain would be an exciting, attractive place for foreign investors.

11. Supporters of the EU claim that if Britain left the EU our economy would quickly die. This is a nonsense for several reasons. First, Britain imports far more goods than it exports to EU countries. If countries such as Germany and France wanted to continue selling us their goods they would have to allow us to continue to sell them the few things we make. Second, many other countries around the world sell goods to the EU without being members of the EU. The truth is that if we left the EU the external tariff on our imports from outside the EU

would disappear. We would gain enormously from this. We could make special trading deals with countries in the Commonwealth – a far more exciting prospect than trading with Eastern Europe. Most of our exports already go outside the EU so we would suffer very little if the EU imposed an external tariff on British exports to Europe. The World Trade Organisation restricts the tariff to a modest 6% so even if we could not negotiate a smaller tariff (as Switzerland has) the damage would be very small.

12. There would be no risk of our being forced into the euro. The euro is a failing currency. When the euro does fail completely the EU will fall apart. There will then be chaos within those countries which have retained their membership. This is an excellent time to leave a sinking ship.

Printed in Poland
by Amazon Fulfillment
Poland Sp. z o.o., Wrocław